Encore

Prize Poems 2011

Edited by

Valerie Martin Bailey

Honorary Chancellors

Joseph Auslander 1960
John Crowe Ransom 1962
Glenn Ward Dresbach 1963
Jesse Stuart 1964
Grace Noll Crowell 1965
Jean Starr Untermeyer 1966
Loring Williams 1968
Harry M. Meachum 1969
John Williams Andrews 1970
August Derleth 1971
William E. Stafford 1972
N. Scott Momaday 1973
Richard Armour 1974
Richard Eberhart 1975
James Dickey 1976
Judson Jerome 1977
John Ciardi 1979
Robert Coles 1981
Richard Shelton 1983
Marcia Lee Masters 1985
Robert Penn Warren 1986
Richard Wilber 1987
William E. Stafford 1990
Rodney Jones 1992
Tess Gallagher 1995
Michael Bugeja 1997
David Wagoner 2000
Maxine Kumin 2002
Naomi Shihab Nye 2004
Li Young Lee 2006
Lewis Turco 2008
Ted Kooser 2010

2011 CONTESTS
Sponsors, Judges, and Winners

EDITOR'S PREFACE

As poets, we leave written legacies of our thoughts—both serious and humorous. We share our hopes, dreams, and ideas as we enrich one another with our writings.

As I prepared this 2011 edition of *Encore,* I was struck by how many times I typed the names of Helen Keith Beaman, Margo LaGattuta, and Theda Bassett. Three of our brightest stars make their last appearance in this edition. I have typed their names many times in the past seven editions of *Encore,* and I am sure the editors who came before me are also familiar with these names because of their years of service as officers, contest judges, sponsors, or contest winners. That makes this edition a special keepsake not only for their families, but also for us, their poetry family. We will read their poems often and remember the contributions they made to our lives and to poetry. This year we also lost our beloved NFSPS Librarian, Peggy Zuleika Lynch. Peggy has faithfully served both her state society and NFSPS for many years, and she will be sorely missed.

My thanks to Contest Chairman Mikki Pennington for sending in beautiful order the poems and information I need to produce *Encore,* making my job much easier. As always, my heartfelt thanks to Michaud L. Lamrouex for diligent proofreading, and many thanks to NFSPS poets for the pleasure of compiling your poetry in this book.

Valerie Martin Bailey
Editor

"To be a poet is a condition, not a profession."
~ Robert Frost

Contest 1 ~ NFSPS Founders Award
First Place

Last Letter from Grandfather

"The innocent and the beautiful have no enemy but time."
~ William Butler Yeats

The Pacific is fractious; this blue grey mare
Does nothing quietly,
She kicks her stall walls even through dreams
She is not still, her legs stand for no rider.

Mona, I have closed your grandmother's west shutters,
The same facing north along the alders.

The wall facing the untamed sea
Still produces that sound, it barely ever stops, rebounding endlessly
The wind's roar over and over the ocean pulls like two horses.

I woke again last night
It was her endless kicking,
Pawing, or my frightened center pounding?
I think her death has left these plaster walls thin.

In the day, coin flip of night,
Her death is no less manageable,
The bleaching sun
Reflects his O in everything
Just as the night moon's expression seems shocked.
The saline ocean gnaws each horse's feed tub,
It ravages and leaves but an oat froth.
The Pacific is no pacifist,
The word is a misnomer for this wild ocean.

A freeze is on the clapboards.
Real tinsel.
Headstrong it kicked through Christmas.
And locked the slush jell to black terror ice.
This manic mare does not like the cold.
And this maniac horse is no pacifist.

I pillowed to smother its nuisance,
Which turns the pulsing rumble
To a dull moon
Softened, but no less constant,
No less incessant.

Mona, I recall your grandmother
On this white beach reading, protected
In the sea dune grasses passing her last days here.
I envision her upright still, and bone-like defiant
Like the toughened straw reeds remaining the winter,
Both woman and plant in a truce with sand and wind.
She with her writing or drawings, or just there quieted.

Your grandmother performed silence
In these sand dune caves.

Each wave she let crash over, and under
With no threat of the impending tomb.
Your grandmother is outlasting even the snow birds,
Her presence remains here in her garden too.

The patch of phlox has overfilled the wall she stacked.
She knew architecture would never hold,
Knew the want of the root's ache.
She knew nothing would cloister its freedom. Its fingers climbed,
Took the fence, and returned to nature.

Her crocuses will birth and endure without thinning this spring,
Without Grandmother's sure white hands
Or prayers knelt along Grandmother's walking stones.

And this will be the first year seeds will drop,
Crack, green, and fruit as orphans,
With no seraphim in a maternal cloak beckoning.
But summer is a long season away,
Many dry months must come to end.
Her garden endured the first wave of blue ice frost.
Just yesterday, glass blanketed some, was a torch to many.

For the first time in seventy years
There will be no worn linens, no frayed coverlets tossed
To quilt the less established,
No frayed linen from the attic cast
To mother the bed nubs against the rule of the unbearable.

The first time there will be no sleepless shadow
At the upstairs window
Spying prayers through the one small pane,
No woman's forceful entreaties
Against the insane wind and weather,
Against the vain tempest.

Love kicks like a horse, its counterpart the sea
Passion is this woman.
She hardly ever recedes from tenacious offerings.

Mona, your grandmother, aged and gray, was sprinkled here
Over the back of the recalcitrant mare, to ride with her forever.
With her there, these chopping caps now froth more white
And bear more witness than the sun face alone
Could ever wish for or happen to offer.

George Handy
Asheville, North Carolina

Contest 1 ~ NFSPS Founders Award
Second Place

Harvest
A Trilogy

I. The Corn

Tan pockets full
the corn waits
row on row
for the mad crescendo
sudden shock
when the picker's fingers
find the stalk
and press, press gold.

II. The Machine

I am Mordor
I am green
with heavy tread
I walk the field.

My yellow eyes
their downward beams
probe whispering cornrows
fields of beans.
Their golden burden
I consume
part husk from corn
and corn from cob.

My food is gas
my blood is oil
I'll go, I'll go
in endless toil.
I like to chew
I like to eat
Husks and pods
of corn and beans.
But just the same

I also love
overalls
and muddy gloves.

And these low clouds
of dingy gray
have followed me
this cursed day.
This leathery stuff
you make me eat
does not sit well
it sickens me.

I soon will have him
I am stopped
in goes his hand
I've got him, Ha!

III. The Yield

There is no question
the man will survive,
but its almost as if
there has been a death,
and no one seems sure of
the right thing to say...

The arm has been sent
from the accident scene
and lies out of sight
behind the curtain.
And the coveralled man,
this still, silent man
is just starting to sense
the great nothingness
flowing down from his shoulder.
Directions continue
to pour through torn nerves
but are lost in the
massive compression dressing
that keeps him alive
as he lies on the cart.

Behind his closed eyelids
the accident happens
again and again, and
he can't change the outcome
each time it replays.
He seems to be caught
in a slow moving time-warp
of frozen reaction
and aftermath.

He suppresses the urge
to vomit, to scream,
to stop this mad dream
as it slowly progresses,
to cover his face
with his hands,
with his hand.

Barbara J. Kalm
Solon, Iowa

Contest 1 ~ NFSPS Founders Award
Third Place

Hoffmann Knows

"The world is beautiful. It's terrible. It's worth knowing."
~ Nobel Prize winner, Roald Hoffmann: chemist, poet, playwright

First he knows wooden blocks,
stacked up so high before they crash.
The urge to push them again
watch them smash against each other.
Three years old when German boots
march through his Polish village,
he comes to know the ghetto as home
and then the labor camp. Skeletons,
he learns, can bend and speak,
sleep with bony fingers
curled close to the cheek.

Smuggled out,
hiding is a game he comes to know.
Game without a finish.
He learns the taste of darkness, dust
in a schoolhouse attic. Knows
other children as scraps glimpsed through the hole
formed by a single crumbling brick.
He can keep a secret, call it
by his own name.

Chorus of times tables ringing
out beneath him, he practices
silence, the art of invisibility.
Tracing digits on his mama's
arm, he memorizes terror.
His father running,
arms rising up, body slowly falling.

Numbers.
of Jewish children from his town,
he's one of three, one
of three
Jewish children still alive
among four thousand.

There are things he knows
he will not tell, and other things
he leans in close to learn: formulas,
chemistry, tricks to neutralize acid.
What's harsh can smooth away,
can purify like pain.

The larger world fades away
as he spirals down, down
into the forming
and breaking of atomic rings.
The smallest things scatter, beads
of a broken bracelet skittering off
to nowhere—then the search for balance,
for bonds that endure.
Chaos and order
shove against each other,
hungry children in line,
parts of an atom.

Elements whirl
an unseen heart and Hoffmann bends
toward them,
boy at the peephole,
calm, attentive
in the center of a fury.
How exhausting, how beautiful,
his concentration, his ability to love,
to find some kind of order, given all he knows.

Ginny Lowe Connors
W. Hartford, Connecticut

Contest 2 ~ Winners' Circle Award
First Place

Ordinary Time

We're on the deck, easy with our drinks,
our faint sunburns, that summer feeling
we've escaped from ordinary time.

They're out at the island, three teenagers
fooling around at the rope swing.
Against the sun we see their silhouettes

swinging back and forth, hear their laughter
and the loud punctuation of young bodies
hitting water. The trick is to swing straight out

and let go at the apex over deep water,
beyond the boulders that lurk
close to shore. One of the boys out at the rope

now swings back and forth, back.
Reluctant to face that brief terror
of hanging onto nothing. A girl in the water

laughs at him, shouts, *Michael, come* ***on****!*
Wind pushes sheets of silver across the lake,
hiding whatever weeds or stones await

beneath the surface. The boy at last lets go—
there's no way to refuse the future.
His splash joins the others and he surfaces

with a shout that sounds like a yodel.
Closer to us, a child's inflatable ball
floats by, twirling and scudding

as the breeze puffs and pauses.
My thoughts take me to a different lake
and I'm a child again, in a boat

with my brother and papa. When my grandpa
falls overboard, half the lake rises up,
the rowboat rocks hard and Papa's hat

floats in the long suspense before
he reappears, spouting water like a whale.
He's a beautiful man, huge in his kindness,

exuberant, clumsy. But somehow
childhood dissolves and now Papa
is an old felt hat floating in my memory.

Beside me my husband puts down his beer,
calls the dog to him and for a quick moment,
hugs him tight. The dog's white-tipped tail

beats like a metronome. Out at the island
the rope swings empty—the kids head for shore.
Rowdy insults carry over the water.

I turn toward my husband and do not say,
O, what will become of us? And I do not say,
I love sharing these moments with you

(oh why, *why* don't I say it?).
Instead I show him the tomatoes,
firm and perfectly ripe. I give him

the fresh fish, ready for grilling.
I slap a mosquito that's stealing
my blood. I chop the basil.

Ginny Lowe Conners
West Hartford, Connecticut

Contest 2 ~ Winners' Circle Award
Second Place

Three Wishes

If I could give you
from the palm
of my hand
three intricate stars of milkweed
because I do not have words
to say what I want to tell you,
instead I would offer you the perfect fibers
of downy silk twirling
across the sky and my open hand,
each star holding the meaning of speechless thought
visible and layered,
white filaments reaching,
and somehow that would be enough,
the transfer from my hand to yours
and all would be understood
as your hand lifted the understanding
level with your eyes—
maybe then as you looked down the soft spindles,
like overlapping threads of time,
you could hear the whisper
of a mother's breath to son,
the gentle wind stirring
the silken chords
to speak
for me.

Jane Pettibone Homan
Littleton, Colorado

Contest 2 ~ Winners' Circle Award
Third Place

Good Karma

On Palmdale Rd., mercury-glass
shadows move through the fog layer.
You grip the steering wheel
and drive on. An oversized
ace of spades blows across the road.
You brake hard, avoiding it.

Pull over and walk,
says a little voice from somewhere.

Around the bend, you stumble
upon a pristine crystal lake.
Lily pads move like helping hands
in its freshwater; silvery minnows
mill around them, swimming
with good karma. Reach for it,
the little voice says.
So you do.

Nancy Ryan
East Greenwich, Rhode Island

Contest 3 ~ Almeda Boulton Memorial Award
First Place

Elegy

A man must work like this, he said.
No other explanation
for his sweat, the lack of words
glistening.

The tools are in the shed as he last left them.
The music plays again
when time or gravity or both
pull rusted metal to the rotting floor.

But the song remains the same.
The handle of the shovel remembers
his rough but steady hold
around its throat, how it learned to sing.

Andrew David King
Hayward, California

Contest 3 ~ Almeda Boulton Memorial Award
Second Place

Earthbound

I'm tired of old bristlecone, the scree,
the callous wind. The pines are stiff and spare.
The roots hold on but fail to satisfy
the tree. I've come to settle under loam
and moss—I'm sure there's room—about a birch,
or aspen, easy trees, their budding leaves,
like edgy love, unsure of sudden green.
I'll sense when wind has churned the clouds
and bruised the sky. I'll hear the cocky sun
crack ground, release the spicy spores that scent
the rain. I'm here for what I've missed—
the worm and mole at home, a solid bed—
not what I know—the quick of love, the moon
full blast, sharp stars, the endless press of time.

Maurine Haltiner
Salt Lake City, Utah

Contest 3 ~ Almeda Boulton Memorial Award
Third Place

The Way Things Are

is how they need to be.
You can't change them
with dice and a Tarot card.
The way things are sings
to you in daylight, just as
sun lifts over a mountain
of sorrow, the last song
of evening before the heavy
thunk of eyelids pulls you

down to the river of dream,
where the way things are
is illuminated by candles
and Scotch tape. You try
to mend the way things are
with scissors and Elmer's
glue, fold and bend it to a
shape you can live with,

confuse it with origami, the
art of folding, the art of folding
your heart into the shape of a
toaster, so that the way things
are becomes crisp, becomes
tasty spread with apricot jam
and eaten for breakfast with tea.

Margo LaGattuta
Rochester, Michigan

Contest 4 ~ Donald R. Stodghill Memorial Award

First Place

Regeneration…

on the beach

Although the sea often spoke to me
about beginnings, I heard only
the requiem cries torn by the wind
from throats of falling seagulls.
And there were shells…
too many shattered shells
and disembodied crab claws
scattered on the sand each morning,
too many bleached skeletons lying
like broken pocket combs
among the tangled clippings
of Medusa's hair.

But this new Atlantic morning,
while the priming sun
pumped blood into the ocean's
pulsing skin, light-footed around
the blue coffins of mussels,
like another stick-legged carrion picker
on the beach, I saw among the carnage
a single hatching sand flea rising
like a Boticelli Venus
from the pearly fragment
of a scallop shell.

Alvin M. Laster
Southbury, Connecticut

Contest 4 ~ Donald R. Stodghill Memorial Award

Second Place

Ode to the Eraser

Little bullet of solace
quicker than a Minute Man,
you defend against insurgencies
of graphite or lead.
Your color irrelevant to quality,
your sexual preference moot,
you are firm but resilient,
patient yet alert.
Once called into service
you accept your assignment
without complaint.

So plainly uniform when new,
you soon surrender the crisp edges of inexperience
to work on, in, behind, between the lines,
get down, get dirty.
Irregular as special forces,
disguised as a tired lump of gum, ugly,
maybe maimed, you bear scars of each skirmish
into the next encounter.

The writer salutes you, embattled one,
counts on your humble loyalty,
your innumerable sacrifices, great and small.
Together you fight against peril,
against letters excessive, disorderly,
against the undisciplined hordes of words,
against poisonous clouds of ill-penned gas.
And when you find yourself
diminished through months of duty,
undecorated, retired, replaced,
rest easy and contented, gallant warrior,
assured your gift of self and substance
is mankind's more than modest gain.

Barbara J. Funke
St. George, Utah

Contest 4 ~ Donald R. Stodghill Memorial Award
Third Place

Sary's Letter

May 24, 1875
Libertyville

To my dear sister Nancy,

At long last I heard from David.
He's been out west in Colorado for going
on two years, 'bout the longest he's stayed
in one place, I expect. I swear he was born
wearing the wrong size shoes, always discarding
one pair after another hoping he would find something
that finally fit. He wrote to tell me he'd been searching
for TRUTH. I know, he just wrote it that way,
all in capital letters like it had been carved
on stone tablets. He heard about the Mormons
out there in Salt lake, so he up and bought
a team of mules, packed off Peachy Ann
and the children (and the baby being just six weeks old!)
cross those fearsome mountains.
For a smart man David has as much sense
as a moth drawn to a candle's flame.
He's so dazzled by the light, he doesn't
feel the heat until everything's ashes.
Though he was mighty impressed
with Mr. Young and felt he had the look of a prophet,
there were certain points of doctrine
he could not abide. It's my opinion
Peachy Ann was afraid he would up and marry
a whole harem of wives. Peachy Ann
can be persistent as a mosquito when she wants.
David says they are back at Petrified Stump
and the ranch will need some fixing up
and he can't find some of the cows

but he knows the Lord will provide.
He always did favor that passage
about the lilies of the field.
I give him another year before
he'll be wanting to try on
another pair of shoes.

Your loving sister,
Sary

Kathryn E. Clement
Mesa, Arizona

Contest 5 ~ Georgia Poetry Society Award
First Place

Green Grass of Happiness

"happy as the grass was green"
from "Fern Hill" by Dylan Thomas

She was as happy as the grass was green
that day in May, untroubled as the sky
was blue. Her eyes were clear, her smile serene;
her beauty caused a soft, collective sigh.
The church was filled, the Georgia day was cool
as Sarah Ann and John McVeigh were wed.
She smiled and raised her floating veil of tulle,
accepting Johnny's kiss when vows were said.
She danced the first cotillion with her groom,
encircling hoops and bouffant skirts awhirl.
She smiled at all the guests around the room,
so happy was this lovely southern girl.
    They started married life with hopeful schemes
    and prayed that war would not intrude on dreams.

The year was eighteen sixty-one and war
was in the air as Sarah Ann and John
began their married life. But long before
the honeymoon was over, John was gone
to fight the Yankees. Sarah Ann was left
to run the big plantation house alone,
to deal with crops and missing slaves and theft
and hardship. Worked her fingers to the bone,
the old folks said. But constant work helped keep
her sanity. Though she was brave and strong,
the lonely nights would often make her weep.
This dreadful war was going on too long.
    It seemed the south would quickly win at first,
    but now they feared the southern cause was cursed.

Still Sarah Ann withstood and every night
she wrote to John, her letters never sad,
attempting to convince him all was right.
She prayed for him, for news of war was bad.

A year had passed since he'd been home on leave,
and half a year since she'd had any word.
But still she wrote, determined not to grieve,
regrdless of the rumors that she heard.
While cotton in the warehouse gathered dust
the barn was burned, the cows released to roam,
and crops destroyed. The war was lost. But just
when times were darkest, John came limping homc.
    Forgetting all the tragic years between,
    she was as happy as the grass was green.

Joyce Shiver
Crystal River, Florida

Contest 5 ~ Georgia Poetry Society Award
Second Place

The Ghosts of Vicksburg

On summer afternoons, a certain haze
will form between the cannons in the park,
and some are certain on those humid days
that thin smoke rises to reveal a stark
and once-embattled officer of Grant
or skirmish-shattered, barefoot Rebel lad.
Photographers snap photos to affirm
suspected specters, others will recant,
believing ghostly sightings to be sad
hallucinations no one can confirm.

This crucial fortress city then controlled
the Mississippi. Far below this bluff
the sullen and forbidding waters rolled.
When several assaults were not enough,
a siege was ordered, As their hunger grew,
the citizens ate dogs and leather shoes.
The garrison soon faltered. No relief
appeared. When union infantries broke through,
the local leaders shuddered at the news,
their pride now pilfered by the Yankee thief.

On Independence Day, the city fell
to overwhelming forces from the North.
For decades, citizens recalled the hell
and cursed their fate each year on July fourth.
They lived with phantoms from a war long lost.
Crushed Vicksburg, haunted by the ghouls of grief,
could not recover. Not all wraiths are mist.
New generations have assessed the cost
and buried apparitions of belief,
though lost dreams that refuse to die persist.

Russell H. Strauss
Memphis, Tennessee

Form: Keatsian Ode

Contest 5 ~ Georgia Poetry Society Award
Third Place

My Cherokee Grandmother

I never heard her chant the morning sun
or sing an ancient blessing on her brood,
until she hummed, her voice an undertone

as if her blessing lasted till the moon
rose high and all the stars dispersed. I said
I never heard her chant the morning sun

but underlying all my work, I drone,
and who's to say the melody, the rude
raw notes I've hummed—my voice an undertone

like hers, as though I resonate—my tongue
and skin retain her syllables. Indeed,
I never heard her chant the morning sun

the wind's strange songs infuse my reedy bones.
My drum of walking lengthens where I stood
until life hums, *her* voice an undertone

of who I am. I feel I'm not alone,
for she's in me a part of all that's good.
I never heard her chant the morning sun
but now, she hums for me, my undertone.

Helen Keith Beaman
Provo, Utah

Contest 6 ~ Poetry Society of Texas Award
First Place

Last Battles

I think of the time that runs through us.
Fanatical ruin, the castle around us:
the tracery window casts intricate shadow.
We move with the wind like these birds, red sandstone
only a coat that we wear.
        You whisper that armor, like birds,
comes home to rust, and I tell you your eyes are the sky.
You insist and you point
        to the peacock wilted with rain.

We walk in the grooved steps. Millions at least before us,
each placing foot after foot on the ramparts' red brimstone.

The wind, your hair, this smell of rain
like the sea: you play your Lancelot to my pondering Arthur,
with the Saxon host balanced before us;
the earl to the churl, we come
to the sound of pipes and bones.
        Heroic, undaunted, we imagine
the work of a claymore leaves stains
to darken darker the sandstone.

        We battle our way out of rain into darkness.
This tower, that war; our classic last stand.
Like an eloquence of slaughter overheard,
the ravens above heave their wings in slategray nothingness:
and some of our friends the gray wolf shares with death.
We try so hard—at times—not to be melodramatic;
we understate cases, we think we go like Cyrano
caparisoned in gems unseen.
        But touring dark ruins where the earth itself is charnel
our little defiance is all that defines.
One last kiss and your hand clenched in mine,
your hair, your clothes, your face wet with glory:

I wonder how desperately we love—each other, *the memento mori*
scratched in the rock, all: the glorious tarnished offal of life.

Later the sun comes.
You stand on the broken tower; below, my telephoto lens
watches you shake in the wind, your dangerous perch on the sandstone.
—Be careful!—I call to you.
But you (o Lancelot, o chevalier!) only laugh.

Jeremy M. Downes
Auburn, Alabama

Contest 6 ~ Poetry Society of Texas Award
Second Place

Burn

They say you can't remember it,
once the pain is over, but I
remember a tulip, deep and red,
a blossom I'd fallen into, its walls
soft and steep. Every time
I tried to climb out, I slipped
tumbling deep into its heart
unforgiving cup of self
solitary, full of heat. And there
I curled up small, spiraled
round and round myself.
The air too close, too sweet.
Waves of light, then darkness
fell over me, and *Surely,*
I thought, *I'm drowning.*

Ginny Lowe Connors
West Hartford, Connecticut

Contest 6 ~ Poetry Society of Texas Award
Third Place

An Invitation from the Moon

The moon, an old woman who answers no questions
and speaks no assurances, rides by the hospital window,
wrapping another shawl around her shoulders each time.
The boy is familiar with such cool silences.
On nights when the moon does not appear,
he believes he sees her shadow,
darker than the dark.

One night, when noises in the hall startle him awake,
the brilliant full moon appears in his window.
There is a secret in everything unseen, he says to himself,
for now the moon is young, and she is smiling.
She tosses a rope of light to earth, and it lands
on the boy's pillow.
Now he is enchanted by what must be
an invitation, for there is nothing
but this radiant pathway between them.
No obstacles at all.

He is certain that the moonbeam rope stretching
from here to her is strong enough to bear his fragile weight.
He reaches out, takes hold,
and pulls himself upward, hand-over-hand.

Janet Watson
Wesley Chapel, Florida

Contest 7 ~ Utah State Poetry Society Award

First Place

Guardians of the Flame

We are the keepers of the fires.
In dreams, our ancestors remind us
of fires burned outside caves and huts
to welcome home the hunter with the kill,
victorious warrior, crusader, sailor.
Legends of our steadfastness have been told
throughout the ages.

We hold lanterns and torches
at land's end; build bonfires on rocky
beaches, as we scan the dark horizon,
unforgiving sea, shadowed forest.
We are the patient sex, crowned with forbearance
that is, at once, birthright and burden.

Our strength is tempered on the pyres
of soldiers carried home on shields, children
lost to famine and disease. We are the earth's
most accomplished mourners—throwing locks
of our hair into the blaze.
In whispers, screams and the eloquent
signing of the heart, we petition—
not for quarter, but endurance.

Placers of lamps and candles,
we keep our window-vigils as untiringly
for prodigal as for returning hero; we await loves'
safe homecoming in silence, but we are not alone.
Around us are the spirits of women who have
sentineled at all the windows of the world.

Tenders of cookfires,
brewers of comfort and healing herb,
we wait for dawn and fever's break with
the same calmness as we await the seasons.
We rock the fretful infant and hum a lullaby
with origins older than recorded history.

Stayers of night, we watch our votives
turn to liquid, as we attend the bedsides
of childbirth and life's passing,
and in the uncertain light that resurrects
each day—*our* flame is sure.

Dian S. Barnett
Marietta, Georgia

Contest 7 ~ Utah State Poetry Society Award
Second Place

Missing the Connection

I have inherited her urge to hang on
to every piece of string, tan or yellow, rubber bands,
keys that no longer fit locks.
Like her I live under an insulating clutter of paper:
stacks on shelves, some with unopened junk mail
piled next to unfiled awards.

I have probably been given her colon
and perhaps even the tendency to grow tumors,
something which will need checking
and rechecking along the way.

I have inherited her handwriting.
My little sister says to the middle one,
"Look, she writes just like Mom."
Our up and down scrawl,
how we both capitalize our Hs and Ps.

We tend to put our dreams under our pillows
and help those close to us reach for stars.

We recognize faces, notice insignificant details
(like when Wendy's counters have changed color).
We talk to strangers in Laundromats,
carry on conversations at the grocery store.

We love watermelon,
drink cream in our coffee,
make dates to eat rice pudding.

We have a fascination for words:
she, the queen of crossword puzzles;
I, a matador of metaphor.

I knit mittens and hats. She crochets afghans
for all the grandkids. We can describe
the buttons and pins on outfits we wore
all the way back to the 1950s.

We baked cakes for each others' birthday,
competed for the same poetry prizes,
and when she died, my delight in her company
died and was buried with her.

Charmaine Pappas Donovan
Brainerd, Minnesota

Contest 7 ~ Utah State Poetry Society Award
Third Place

Lest We Forget

"...houses full of good things...and wells digged, which thou diggedst not, vineyards and olive trees, which thou plantedst not...beware lest thou forget..." Deuteronomy 6:11-12

I drink from wells I did not dig,
reap harvests I did not plow,
tread golden fields rich from the sweat
that cleansed the weathered brow.

I sift clean dirt through lily hands
where the calloused extracted stones,
quench fruited groves from channels carved,
plant seed over crops once sown.

I gaze on breathless mountain heights
made tame by fearless feet,
whisper words I did not pen,
sing anthems on velvet seat.

Draw shade by trees I did not set,
pick grapes from plaited vines,
taste honey from bees whose industry
sculpts this Eden of mine.

My wrist carries pulse with faithful beat,
blood runs from ancestral springs,
my heart turns to Headwaters
on shoulders, I stand with wings.

Julie Nelson
Orem, Utah

Contest 8 ~ Florida State Poets Association, Inc. Award
First Place

Sarah Cunningham

I was raised at the trading post west of Cortez.
With my thick black hair and dark eyes,
no surprise the Navajos
claimed me as their own.
They called me *nizhoni,* beautiful,
fed me fry bread and mutton stew,
but then I grew up and away from them.
Taught school until I married a dreamer.
With our brood that finally numbered seven,
I followed him from Tonapah to Silver City,
From Butte to Pecos to Santa Fe,
until one hot day in Tucson, he left me
for a dancing girl with yellow hair
and died of the influenza that fall.
Regrets? Oh, yes indeed.
I was never happy white.

Joyce Kohler
Midway, Utah

Contest 8 ~ Florida State Poets Association, Inc. Award
Second Place

Arthur Thompson

Sure, I was always the runt,
the little guy bullies picked
on. All the girls laughed the day
Tom Hess pulled my pants
off and tossed them in the river.
He even stole my lunch money
more than once.
No one ever helped me until Sean
FitzMorris came to our school.
He told Tom and his friends
to leave me alone.
Sean was so big no one
wanted to try him. Everything
was fine until the night of Senior
Prom. On my way home,
Tom, George Gentry, and some
other boys beat me up and took
all of my clothes. That night Tom
left this life in pieces, torn apart
by Grandpa's old shotgun.
No one was laughing then.
Sean was the only one who came
to see me. He told me God
still loved me, but I knew better.

Eric H. Read
Brigham City, Utah

Contest 8 ~ Florida State Poets Association, Inc. Award

Third Place

Felix Seeley

Now there are special classes for those like me—
"Special-needs" people.
That sounds so much kinder than the harsh terms
Of my day—"retarded" and "not all there."
Most "normal" people in town really loved me;
Others simply couldn't hide their pity.
While those around me went to school and college,
Played their sports, joined the clubs,
Married, had families, and went to work,
I learned from them, my family, and the town.
As I loved the Lord and people, laughed, lived,
And grew wise in my own way,
I observed some who lived good lives—
Busy, but not too busy to care and listen.
From my sheltered spot, I watched others
As they multi-tasked, made money, got promotions,
Built big houses, and drove expensive cars,
But never really listened to anyone
Except superiors, who demanded their allegiance.
They failed to care until they couldn't care.
Pity "normal" people with hardened hearts,
Unseeing eyes, and unhearing ears—
The ones who pity those like me.

Janice Canerdy
Potts Camp, Mississippi

Contest 9 ~ Alabama State Poetry Society Award

First Place

Confession of a Firstborn Girl, A Virgo with a Red Personality and Mormon Parents

If not for the above,
I'd live on an island with unpaved roads
where people speak in a foreign tongue—a nod, a wave.
All day I'd watch the ocean,
and one evening when I could think no more
about what I should have done, or been,
or not done,
I'd wade out into the slanting light,
the shallow surf,
    saltiness and the sea's lapping song
    soothing my perilous need to be right,
                                        to be best,
                                        to be enough for them and him.

An emptied shell, I'd float away
and they, they would all say,

if only she'd been the second child,
more accustomed to following,

or a son, with more windows to look out.

Perhaps a Pisces. They swim like fish.
Virgos are so earthbound.

If she'd been more yellow than red, more forsythia, arms extended,
less rose, fists one day, palms open the next.

If her parents had been agnostic,
If she'd grown up questioning God, instead of herself.

Elaine W. Christensen
Sandy, Utah

Contest 9 ~ Alabama State Poetry Society Award

Second Place

A Happening in Spring

From just inside a glass-paned door, we watched
spring's tentative arrival…a pair of house wrens
returned to the familiar—a gourd-shaped planter
they'd borrowed before. Scratching and tossing
winter-brown things, they created a cradle of twigs
and grasses and skeletal leaves, pieces of string
and thread, layered soft with found bits of cotton
and discarded feathers—the gathered leavings of
nature and human presence.

At last, one of them settled, a scant half-ounce
of feathered instinct, quiet and still as a carving,
warming something of value beneath. In benign
trespass when both birds were away, we moved
near, to peer at a grace of dappled eggs…
Within vigilant days, we heard new life stir and
trumpet its sounds. Four downy nestlings
announced their presence, crowding out winter,
hurrying spring.

Four hungry beaks were opened wide, their
small sounds louder with each parent's approach.
Swiftly the pair flew their missions; returning with
small-insect feedings gently pressed into yawning
beaks. Three slender days of early spring, two
small wrens nurtured new life, and renewal
chorused its glory song.

Then, sharp-eyed, quizzical, flitting about in
abberant patterns, criss-crossing the airspace of a
covered porch, they hovered like hummingbirds,
just above their huddled brood—their perfect
young—soft sculptures now, and strangely silent
before they had a chance to sing… As flies
gathered and circled, two paired wrens flew away
from death.

Sweet God of new beginnings—why? . . How shall I vindicate this burial—this shibboleth of a silent spring?

Jeanne Couvillon-Powell
Spring Texas

Contest 9 ~ Alabama State Poetry Society Award
Third Place

Lifeless

When my friend slumped
to the floor at sixty-six,
lifeless as the dust cloth
in her hand,
a crimson explosion
in her head
taking charge,
I was stunned anew
at how unpredictable
irreversible
inevitable
death is.

This morning I whacked
a tiny fly
on the bathroom mirror,
mashed the works
of its amazing body,
flattened the black veil
of miraculous wings
against silvered glass,
saw it all
reflected right back
at me.

Janet Henderson
Windsor, Connecticut

Contest 10 ~ Connecticut Poetry Society Award
First Place

A Lesson in Trust at the Feet of Millet
An ekphrastic poem in the Gloss form

"These children and the mother and a bowl—
here is the scene which circumscribes my soul.
Fledglings of peace whose need is their defense—
these are my insights into innocence."
~ Jessica Power, from her poem
*Millet's "Feeding Her Birds"**

These children and the mother and a bowl—
their father labors nearby in the field,
while mother worked before dawn turning yield
into a breakfast. Their young stomachs growl
as they sit feasting there among the fowl,
these children and the mother and a bowl.

Here is the scene that circumscribes my soul.
How patiently their mother must have toiled
to turn to sustenance these gifts of soil.
How eagerly her children, like young birds,
beg for their share without the use of words—
here is the scene that circumscribes my soul.

Fledglings of peace whose need is their defense—
these little ones depend on Mother's care.
She hears the cupboard's warning—it is bare;
knows every dance of weather that can steal
the promised crop. She's thankful for this meal.
Fledglings of peace whose need is their defense—

These are my insights into innocence.
With hungry eyes, the trusting little flock,
expects each ample meal around the clock.
These naïve little hatchlings cannot guess
the fragile tree beneath the family nest.
These are my insights into innocence.

Lisa M. Salinas
Spring, Texas

**La Becquée* (literally "Beakful"), the name of the 1860 painting by Jean-François Millet, has been translated into English in various ways. Jessica Powers chose to refer to it as "Feeding Her Birds." The painting is located at *Palais des Beaux-Arts de Lille in Lille, France.*

Contest 10 ~ Connecticut Poetry Society Award
Second Place

Life in an Apron
(Grant Wood's *American Gothic*)

The traveling photographer came today.
I never wanted my picture taken,
but Caleb insisted.
Four years married and still no babies,
but five of Caleb's children to raise,
and bad-mannered children they are too.
Of course, Caleb's no sugarplum, either.

But why the pitchfork?
We *are* farmers,
but do we need the pitchfork?

I don't have time to stand here
in the sweltering sun
while the photographer,
looking like a blind hangman,
crawls under the black hood,
back out,
tells us not to move,
don't smile,
moves under again.

I have bundles of laundry to wash,
floors to clean,
bread to bake,
butter to churn.

My life wasn't supposed to be like this.
I planned for adventure like in the stories.
I saw myself buying spices in an Arabian bazaar,
testing silks in China,
dancing in Paris,
attending the opera in Milan.

Instead, I live my life in an apron,
my hair pulled into an untidy bun.
I'm a slave instead of a princess.

But who knows?
Maybe this picture is my chance for fame.

Joyce Shiver
Crystal River, Florida

Contest 10 ~ Connecticut Poetry Society Award
Third Place

What We Hunger For

Based on the painting "The Angelus"
by Jean Jacques Millet

Red sky dances doom
across parched land.
Father, mother,
their head bowed,
plead for deprived fields
to surrender one more time.

A famine-engulfed country
wrings her people dry,
leaves them hard as the ground
whose veins meander, mirroring
lines on a withered map.

Painted out of sight, I imagine
children waiting in a thatched-roof,
weathered hut.

They resemble stick figures
scratched on a chalkboard
by a teacher too hurried
to draw flesh on hungry bones.

At dusk, kneeling around
a rough-hewn table,
the humble family pronounces
gratitude for the day's
meager gleanings—
a few stunted potatoes—
enough for soup.

Today, ours is a different kind
of famine.
We pray to Wall Street...
ask for more.

Karen Gibson
Provo, Utah

Contest 11 ~ Max & Beverly Keith Golightly Memorial Award
First Place

Dancing Fingers—Fossil, Wyoming

"Since...hearing the tick-tick-tick of the telegraph instrument,
I had a desire to know how to talk with my fingers."
Alma Ellis journel—1908

Are you lonesome, Mr. Dancing Fingers,
your only partner the lower platinum point
of a telegraph key? As your hand dashes
left, dots right, in a slow-click-click foxtrot,
steps light as prairie dust, words easy
as love at first sight, do you imagine someone's daughter
in town counting your footsteps, her manner shy
as a bee before the plunge into pollen? You
transcribe twenty-five words per minute—near
warp speed for 1905. Each page sent, received, terse,
stopped. Nothing novel. Chance an ignored
beggar in this railroad station nowhere
in Wyoming. Except the earth

beneath your feet, fifty-four million years ago,
approximately, was lake bottom. Why do you
never stoop in April sunshine to gather a slice
of fossil shale? Tempered millions of years before
redemption, powdered with limestone, their chocolate
outlines remain sure as luck. They speak
for God. Your fingers would spark with invisible
voltage, receive transmissions from dry limbo—the fuss
of paddlefish, alligator grumbles, even sighs
from restless palm fronds. But you overlook
His words. Forget "Carpal Tunnel, Operator
Paralysis, Writer's Cramp, Glass Elbow," a frenzy
of names for rhythmic dyslexia. You see nothing
electrifying to report. Your fingers are hushed.
Fossil Butte sleeps. Beyond your window, moonlight
crashes on limestone.

Maurine Haltiner
Salt Lake City, Utah

Contest 11 ~ Max & Beverly Keith Golightly Memorial Award
Second Place

If The Moon Can Float

If night can hunker like a thief
in the foothills,
waiting to steal tree by tree
across the valley,
then I can kneel, an old woman
in a dark room,
prayers spiraling up the chimney,
curling themselves in the coils of God's ears.

If prayers can escape
through layered shingles of my roof,
through chinks in brick walls,
then I can hide here, a velvet mole,
safe from the yellow beak,
bent and sharp,
the flapping wings,
that floodlight moon.

If the moon can float all night in the lake,
like a thin smile,
an empty canoe,
God's all seeing eye almost shut,
then I can swim out into the black stream,
a tiny minnow,
a flash of quicksilver,
one fish in a school of stars.

If stars can blink on in the dark
like street lamps,
if street lamps can pool their light
on every corner like gold coins,
if gold coins can link their profiles
into shining bracelets
across the city,
then I can face morning,
arms outstretched,
palms open,
fingers extended,
each, a ray of sun.

Elaine W. Christensen
Sandy, Utah

Contest 11 ~ Max & Beverly Keith Golightly Memorial Award
Third Place

What I Wish I'd Said to the Cop Who Pulled Me Over for Speeding on a Highway Somewhere in Central Kentucky

Look, my longing for companionship extends to the road.
Out here, where cell phones don't connect
and if you're out of gas, you're out of luck,
I only wanted to be part of the pack,
to stay beside the Pepsi truck, a blue Voyager,
the two teens in the Mazda with bumper stickers
for bands I don't know. I wanted the warmth of weaving
in and out of the two lanes as if we four were ice skaters,
compelled by the limits of our cars to remain almost as one.

But officer, the Voyager pulled off
so the driver could examine a map,
the two teens drove faster than I dare,
and the truck slowed down to inch its way somewhere
the driver obviously didn't want to go.
We all know that feeling, right?

All I wanted, sir, my foot pressing down,
was to catch up with someone to coast with,
someone who would allow me to wonder
what their vanity plate stands for,
or if they like the color of their car.
I imagine you get lonely out here, too,
sir, and you look like the kind of man
who wants to know if I believe that where
I am going is better than any place I've ever been.

Mary Christine Delea
Oregon City, Oregon

Contest 12 ~ League of Minnesota Poets Award

First Place

Mother's Dictionary

Words are not mirrors now,
just scrambled symbols
that boggle her wizened wit
as speech falls apart.
She may be losing sound,
but sound is losing sign,
so we are losing touch—
as if our fingers slide apart,
their rips struggling to arc a charge
across the widening gulf.
Michelangelo's ceiling flashes eloquently:
Adam's link to God stretched so thin
their sundered fingers curled
toward themselves
and doused the light.

The Lord's Prayer—
engraved more clearly than her name—
we recite while cheek to cheek,
as if the movement of my face were cue enough.
Alone, her jaw works its hinges;
cords vibrate, tongue undulates;
words halt at hyphens and syllables are orphaned.
This seems a Helen Keller darkness
without an Annie Sullivan miracle.

Shipwrecked, swamped,
we pitch in this mortal storm,
consonants and vowels tossed up
like spray that shocks our faces
before it trickles with tears,
the silver slivers of glass
that cut the eyes and heart,
but not the night.

If I were Lord and every word my own,
commanding her to stand and walk
and speak,
would she then understand
and heed?
Restored, she might yet turn
to these pages of her dictionary
at some inevitable hour.

Barbara J. Funke
St. George, Utah

Contest 12 ~ League of Minnesota Poets Award
Second Place

If Picasso Had Come to Church

Did you know Picasso loved painting doves,
their roundness, their ruffled wings?
He seldom used the color white in his studies,
but it was restful between his 'blue period'
and the 'rose period.'

Yesterday in church
a man spoke from the pulpit, telling us too much,
how he was a sissy as a boy,
how his brothers never let him win.
It was hard to look at him.

Picasso would have liked the blue light
from the stained glass windows
that dappled the man's skin
and would have painted him,
his head fallen to one side,
his head bent like a swan's.
his mouth, two shades of blue, sliding off the edge of his profile.
his eyes, gone from rubbing them with his fists.

The man said self-loathing had brought him to God,
that if he'd been happy, he might never have prayed.

Picasso would have him kneeling
and somehow, a dove, or a ray of light,
or angels' voices would be portrayed.
I like to think he would have given the man all three:
the dove perched on the kitchen sink,
light filtering through a crack in the ceiling,
and Gabriel's horn standing in a corner,
or better, here and there, on the plank flooring,
even caught in the fabric of his suit,
feathers,
large, almost translucent.

Elaine W. Christensen
Sandy, Utah

Contest 12 ~ League of Minnesota Poets Award

Third Place

Paper Boats

I make paper boats
to follow random currents,
slip silently down flooded gutters
into gaping storm drains,
and whirl on backwater eddies.

I send them light and skipping—
ski boats ripping through dawn
across polished lakes.

I send them slow and still—
windless frigates foundering
on outcropped thoughts.

I send them budding and abundant—
flower flotillas spreading out
like green sea bloom.

I make paper boats
to ferry vital bits of me—
a taste for dark chocolate,
a preference for deep red,
an eddying, deep-water faith—

because a hundred years downstream,
you are waiting
for messages on the water.

Merrijane Rice
Kaysville, Utah

Contest 13~ Two Ladies from Texas Award

First Place

Gimmel the Dreidle Cat

Gimmel the Cat does his two legged dance
trying to catch the dangling treat.
When lying down on his left side, it's *hay.*
When lying down on his right side, it's *nun.*
If he sits, satisfied, it's *shin,* we give in.
If he walks around, it's *gimmel,* he won.
He plays as long as coins glitter and clink,
and treats twirl, a gambling cat
who wins eight nights of center stage
—our rescued feline. Gimmel plays
like a *zaide,*pretending not to care,
never lost all, never wants more.

Rosemary Dunn Moeller
St. Lawrence, South Dakota

Contest 13 ~ Two Ladies from Texas Award
Second Place

Poetry for Two

At seventy I memorize a poem
or two for exercising synapse gaps.
With Patch cat near I pull up Oliver.
Her black bear paws my brain. Next, songs
from Merwin's flute. Patch knows the words.
His furry brown-and-white rubs up and down
my legs in sync with nouns and verbs. He purrs
his pleasure for the fading star, the bear
whose blackness dazzles night. He loves this world,
can think no other. Still, when I say *bear,*
does he hear *mouse*? When I say *star,* does he
think *stair*? I finish off the lines. The words
still recognize their place inside my head.
I'm satisfied. Patch knows his poem is next.

He's brought a squeaky play mouse for his text.
It's his delight. "Now throw," he says, through eyes
that shine. This routine his not mine. I toss
the mouse. Patch bounds down stairs and chomps with teeth
I've never felt. I turn. The mouse is back.
I know the rhythm of this game. The verse
is free, all memorized. No stops. The verbs
are Patch. The adjectives are brown-and white.
His poetry recharges all my days.

Maurine Haltiner
Salt Lake City, Utah

Contest 13 ~ Two Ladies from Texas Award
Third Place

Warmed Toes

Her toe predicts the coming on of storms
and reaching cold fronts nearing in the night.
She doesn't measure up to any norms,
but lives alone with just her old cat, Dwight.
She speaks to him, assured he understands
(though Dwight's been deaf for over seven years).
He's learned to pay attention to her hands
and as she rubs her toe he slowy nears
then stretches out across her feet. They sleep
and dream of days when both could run and leap.

Gail Teachworth
Crystal River, Florida

Contest 14 ~ Jesse Stuart Memorial Award
First Place

Meeting My Adult Child

You turned a corner with sharp edges.
It tore off the clothes of childhood
and left them in a heap.
But you continued to walk forward
leaving bare footprints
in the grass.

I heard your voice
above all the hopscotched rhymes
left on the playground years ago.
It spoke of dreams
in a language I barely knew,
but it was your voice
and each word was strong.

Your hands parted the air
with swift strokes as you walked.
They opened to every
ragged shutter
hanging in the alleys of the world.
I thought you would let go of my fingers
gradually,
but it was sudden and swift.

Now we are shoulder to shoulder
like planets who nod to each other
orbiting through the dark.
I am a silent parent
letting you speak first.
It is enough to realize that
from now on,
you can reach the same stars that I can.

Catherine Moran
Little Rock, Arkansas

Contest 14 ~ Jesse Stuart Memorial Award
Second Place

Thirst for Light

Waves roll out and withdraw
untying the night.
Sun skates over the lake,

leaves light
in its wake, infuses
each wrinkle with revelation.

Can we divine ripples,
perceive them, hold them
in the palm of the mind?

With cupped hand,
dip liquid radiance
that leaks over edges,

between fingers
before we can drink.
Thirst returns for children

of the desert, tongue
and cheeks so dry
they bond together,

cause words to falter,
crave moisture
like a drought hankers for rain.

I open my mouth,
sip silver droplets,
imbibe the Word,

utter all I had never
known, never heard.

Helen Keith Beaman
Provo, Utah

Contest 14 ~ Jesse Stuart Memorial Award
Third Place

Recipe for Dragonfly Chicken

First, you must steal a chicken
From the missionaries, they will forgive you,
Maybe not.

You must snare dragonflies, two dozen or more.
Use the thinnest of hair, tie the smallest pebbles
At each end.

You must deceive dragonflies, make them
Think stones thrown into air seem
Flies to eat.

You must catch blues and greens, they make
You swift, courageous, strong.
Let go the reds.

Next, you must dig a pit, build a fire—
Hot, gleaming coals, enough to last
Till dusk.

You must gather onion, lemongrass, cilantro;
Stuff them into the chicken,
Dragonflies, too.

You must wrap this in banana leaves,
Pack with river mud, bury in the
Pit of coals.

Last, you must bake it till dark, when
Dragonflies pin to reeds for the night—
They must not see you eating.

Aaron E. Holst
Sheridan, Wyoming

Contest 15 ~ Indiana State Federation of Poetry Clubs Award
First Place

Practice Makes

All day we practice letting go.
How we hope the cherries
will be riper. But they're not.

How we almost catch the pitcher
of water before it spills. But we don't.
How loved ones seem farther away

than a phone call. How contentment
skirts in the shadows of trees, then
rushes away when we enter the glade.

That is not to say there was not happiness
today. The long swim in the river. The pulling
of weeds along the fence's edge. How

neat the garden rows looked then!
And how red blushed the skin on my lower back
where once again I did not wear sunscreen.

Sigh. And I try to let it go. But there are unseen hooks
in everything, how they catch and snag and cling
to what we thought we wanted, or thought we had to have,

and we are tugged. Stuck. We are burrs in the hems of the day.
not yet able to perfect our fall from imagined grace—
like the perfect way the sun falls with no hitch.

no hindrance, no drag. We are learning to fall,
to fall like that, holding on to nothing, held by nothing.
And part of me believes it could happen—that we could be

content with things as they are. And part of me
fashions new hooks for my sleeves
and sharpens the waiting barbs.

Rosemerry Wahtola Trommer
Placerville Colorado

Contest 15 ~ Indiana State Federation of Poetry Clubs Award
Second Place

What Is Here, What Was There
(Circa 1943)

I never thought about war until
it unhinged the door of our house, a whirlwind
revisiting its path, as greedy as the grave.
Brothers you think you hate going off
one at a time. The house solemn, everyone
holding to the porch rail like blind persons.
Sisters weeping empty beds.

We talked about it, Susan and I, after closing
desks at CQ Headquarters, the Staff Sergeant
with the slight limp looking down
from his elevated home-front position;
after reading letters from Mamas,
I in the upper bunk to ease Susan's phobia:

Why would we think of war, living
in a world made for us? Depression scars
healed, a job rattling our pockets. Twenty,
beautiful, choosy, beating off the boys…

But the boys were gone. The letters that came
had holes in them—boys fighting a war
they couldn't talk about, talking of home.
Guilt sat beside me at the breakfast table—
the Julian boy's name in reports, then others—
by nightfall, every newspaper like a cemetery.

I never thought of war either till Mama
draped the windows in black.

Evelyn Corry Appelbee
Henderson, Texas

Contest 15 ~ Indiana State Federation of Poetry Clubs Award
Third Place

Laughing at Gilded Butterflies

What the fool does at the end,
the wise one does in the beginning.
~ Spanish Proverb

My hands fold and cut, fold and cut.
The blades of my scissors have recalled
the design of butterfly wings.
Enchantment flutters
from strings in the window.
Snow masks the backyard.
Today it is not necessary to admit
tomorrow the sun will rise,
the rose has faded,
and some of us become lunatics.
Saying Big or Little, the child
keeps handing me sheets of paper.
Now I am four years old.
My father is helping me color
the picture of a home with a garden.
He is working. He pauses
every time I point to a different flower.
He says the name of a color.
I run to the table and fill in the correct shade.
Sometimes I go back with two green pieces.
He looks at both and picks the correct one.
It is hard to color the little butterfly.
My father puts down his work,
picks up a brilliant orange
and does not go outside the lines.
When we both finish,
he tears the page from the book
and tapes it to the refrigerator.
This silvery day, my ephemeral collection
of cutout remembrances
takes wing and orbits a universe
where crayons stay inside the lines
and the rose never fades.

When gentle winds stirred
in the graveyard last summer,
kaleidoscopic silk wings hovered
over tiny pastel flowers
blooming above my father's grave.

Rose Ann Spaith
Columbus, Ohio

Contest 16 ~ Arizona State Poetry Society Award
First Place

You Ask How Old Am I…

Air is so still a leaf suspends midway,
its absence from the stoic tree unnoticed.
The brown-toned lawn that will apply
the accepted ritual of life with next April's
gaudy painting of crimson clover
wears its cloak of death like a cozy conflux
of stillness and silence.

The day is awash, the hour flat, as colorless
as a child's lost crayons. The rain gauge
suspends, dependent on more than itself
for its half-full, half-empty state.

I know this room too well. Its walls
rise up like old friends returned from death
to warm cold dreams. This table
moves its legs to my comfort,
its scrubbed face reflects the shadow
of a burned-out candle
and the book I hold that groans
from too many readings.

A nebulous pane permits binoculars.
I count the feathers on the wings
of a late lark as it stirs the stillness
with a yawn. One berried limb
of the Holly tree stirs, and another.
The suspended leaf lifts,
begins its descent to the peaceable bed
of its brothers,

and the earth responds, jarred
by the simple answser.

Evelyn Corry Appelbee
Henderson, Texas

Contest 16 ~ Arizona State Poetry Society Award
Second Place

The Art of Seeing

On my hand I wear the future—
not just in lifelines but in a crystal
ball ring I bought at Spuds gift shop
in Gaylord. When I look into the clear
globe, I can't see much of anything
but my own face. Ahh, so I too
will be in my future. That's a good

thing. I also see a lot of ceilings,
which tells me there will be a ceiling
wherever I am in the coming years—
a lid on things, so to speak. My
future will be contained, not diaphanous
like so much of my past remains.

But I want to know what's going
to happen. I tell the ring as I
politely gaze deep into its glass.
Scrying they call it, or the art of
seeing what hasn't happened yet.

It's a way of moving forward
while I'm still standing here,
a way of knowing what to look
out for as it arrives right now—

but that's a now, not a future.
Maybe there is no such thing,
since all time moves in a circle
and now is always happening
at once, being so stuck on itself
it can't let go and travel forward
or back. My ring says I'm too

nosy and should let my life reveal
itself as it always will, one artichoke
at a time. *The future is hurrying ahead*
and gets lonely for me, I say. *Can't I*

keep it company? Can't I play with it
and teach it tricks? No, says my ring,

you will scare the future away with
your questions. It has a mind of its
own and won't come when it's called,
like a Siamese cat. You can't hold it in your
hand. Please ignore it, and it will come
to you, purring in its own good time.

Margo LaGattuta
Rochester, Michigan

Contest 16 ~ Arizona State Poetry Society Award
Third Place

I Refuse to Participate in Any More Mondays

That plastic cube yapping at me to get up in the dark—
I want to crush it. I fear I'm turning mechanical,
becoming an imperfect machine, with parts that aren't reliable.
I enter the workday resentful.

The odor of indoor heating breaks over me like a rash.
To enter an office, carrying coffee in a brown paper cup—
surely I wasn't born for this.
I just want to eat slices of mango in bed, flip through the news,
return to my dream of the yellow finches.

When I strap myself into my metal cage,
grip the wheel and follow a broken line with the others
all my edges blur, my colors drain out like dish water.

I told my guidance counselor I'd be a beach comber.
When did I become so responsible?

I'm sick to death of improvement committees
data teams, flow charts. I want
the magnificent shock of a meteor blazing toward us,
cratering the golf course, Businessmen scattering.
all that clipped grass blown to smithereens.

How glorious it would be to ride a white horse through the mall.
How fine to hoist myself high on a flag pole
and toss magnolia blossoms down at noon.
Let the mayor catch one in his hair.
Let the superintendent of schools swoon a little
leaning into that soft petaled rain.
Let her shred all the test scores.

Last summer a kid in a paddleboat churned the length of the lake
flying a blue kite, its long tail streaming behind.
Grant that child an exemption from Mondays.

Grant me a chance to become that kite, dipping once, twice
toward the water, then rising till the string gives out,
feeling the hard tug, quiver of tension, and then
breaking free. Let me fall into the updrafts.

Ginny Lowe Connors
W. Hartford, Connecticut

Contest 17 ~ William Stafford Memorial Award

First Place

Renegotiation

It's hard to breathe within the space created by never.
~ Rick Rigsby ~

It's hard to breathe within the space created by never,
fill the lungs with emptiness,
live with a heart pumping dismal predictions.
But look at Rick, running through life
with success on his heels,
kicking gravel at committee members
of the "they said, you can't," statistical society.

He altered cicumstances' dark suit,
ripped condemning *should* seams,
replaced grim buttons with a gold zipper
shining like a medal,
and monogrammed his cuffs with
Don't tell me it's impossible.

Here I am in lipstick redder than a harlot's,
flirting with the same board he fled from,
skirt lifted as though confidence is a garter,
pleading for a recall on my childhood.

I want to renegotiate destiny's terms,
rezone some forbidden boundaries—
pick plums from my neighbor's tree,
play outside past dark and break
criticism's rotten teeth.

I want to learn to tie a double-knot
in the type of thick hairy rope
neighborhood kids used to hang old car tires on.

I want to tuck my body in the belly of one of those old tires
then swing until I am back in my mother's womb,
right before the moment of my birth.
This time when the mid-wife says push,

I would come out swinging, pitch my legs
above clothesline poles, fear, condemnation,
and kick my heels past the world's invisible fence.

Loretta Diane Walker
Odessa, Texas

Contest 17 ~ William Stafford Memorial Award
Second Place

An Artist's Portrait
Observations from behind the sales counter of an art supply store

Artists have paint on their pants,
clay under their fingernails,
always something more important
on their minds than what they are doing now.

They cannot help but dance when the radio
is playing a song they know. Anointed
with linseed oil, dusted in charcoal,
they measure in hand widths and fingers,
leave a trail where they walk of crushed
pastels, would walk on water if they
didn't have to get their feet wet.

Artists work on paper bags, doodle
on the sales counter, doodle over wine
and cheese, have trouble framing
their thoughts. Those who have hair
don't comb it, keep glasses in their pockets,
flirt with fortune, brush with disaster.

Most have no faith in money
ignorant of its religion, unfamiliar
with its various denominations.
Their children are canvases or painted
wood. They change diapers of pallet paper
mounded high in Raw Umber,
all the while not knowing where
their best work may be scattered
all over town like orphans or graffiti.

Shaped like scarecrows with souls
like fat Buddhas, artists see people naked
through their clothes, make them look
better than cameras or mirrors,
leave unimportant things out
of the landscape, hear songbirds
behind the barn, taste the dawn
behind the sunset, and never remember
where they last parked their car.

Anthony (Tony) Fusco
West Haven, Connecticut

Contest 17 ~ William Stafford Memorial Award
Third Place

Ambush

A shriek that could be mistaken
for glee, for a missile, for squealing brakes
breaks the drone of radio talk
and heated wind inside my mobile cocoon.
Deer leap from a hillock obscured by fog,
stumble onto country road.
Right fender and right haunch near-miss.
Ambushed, I feel the kick of hoof on steel.
In the rearview mirror they prance,
brash as fashion models,
scornful of their audience.
One casually swings her cinnamon head
toward my car's gray blur,
this hornless silver specter
that haunts the meanderings of her morning.
A check for damage yields no mark,
but these two ghost guerillas rattle my nerves.
Months of defensive driving mark the hill
and valley there—fogged often, camouflaged and dim—
evoke held breath and tightened grip.

This route's a war zone between dread and duty.
Deer rocket from the roadside at passing vehicles.
Their kamikaze migrations focus fear
but do not force invaders from the field.
I am bound and cannot yield or flee
when, along that road, a flash of dusk-lit doe—
straining caramel over bone and sinew—
blasts past my windshield, steals the right of way,
vanishes like a thief into the brush.
Always in pairs, guerillas have me spooked…

as much as one of two sealed envelopes
set near me on the seat,
one to the War; one coming home.

Will I recount this ambush to my son?
I hug his flimsy letter to my chest.
The worst of armor, its sand-colored sheets
are folds where unknown terrors lurk.

I go on, foot soft on the gas,
hands ten and two,
head and heart on alert.

Barbara J. Funke
St. George, Utah

Contest 18 ~ Nevada Poetry Society Award
First Place

Uneasy in the Dark
Cinquain Sequence

Today
the call of geese
disturbed my sleep, as frost
sought refuge from the creeping edge
of dawn.

I rose
to sapphire sky
and topaz air that stirred
the barnyard to a primal need
to leave.

Fat ducks
and bantam hens
raised their eyes to the "v"
and felt their own wings spread to catch
the breeze.

All day
they watched the clouds
and followed sun, until
long shadows called each feather home
to roost.

Tonight
they stir in sleep.
Uneasy in safety.
Dreaming great heights. Their restless hearts
soaring.

Budd Powell Mahan
Dallas, Texas

Contest 18 ~ Nevada Poetry Society Award
Second Place

On the Edge of the Marsh

Two ducks,
four baby ducks
behind, drift noisclcssly,
a small flotilla slipping down
the creek.

Turtles,
aligned on logs
along the muddy bank
bask in the early summer sun,
at rest.

A great
blue heron stands,
one leg extended, poised,
alert to spear his dinner with
his bill.

The peace
is broken then.
An alligator slides
into the water, drifting down
the creek.

Turtles,
the fleet of ducks,
the great blue heron, too,
and even fish, all disappear
as one.

Joyce Shiver
Crystal River, Florida

Contest 18 ~ Nevada Poetry Society Award

Third Place

Southern Woods

The woods
are mossy-green
where fiddle ferns are curled
around a spring of shimmering
water.

A doe
with frisky fawn
approaches crystal pool
and waits while spotted baby sips
a drink.

The breeze,
that flutters leaves
and makes the pine trees sing,
is jasmine-sweet with just a hint
of mint.

The sky
Is lilac-blue,
where wild canaries fly
with yellow feathers glimmering
like gold.

A howl
of timber wolf
disturbs the peaceful scene,
and frightened deer go scampering
to hide.

In dreams,
Alaskan snow
turns into Southern woods,
and freezing winds are sweet with wild
jasmine.

Kitty Yeager
Arkadelphia, Arkansas

Contest 19 ~ New York Poetry Forum Award
First Place

The Wizard's Guide to Writing a Poem

Use a quill feather
that you cut yourself
dipped in manatee tears
and darkened with thistledown ash.
Translate bird song, frog chorus
and wind sounds in a chimney.
Put it in a bottle
with a willow wand
and a spray of toadflax.
Seal it with the wax of bees
and float it in the reeds
for discovery, like Moses
by the pharoah's daughter.

Arnold Perrin
Union, Maine

Contest 19 ~ New York Poetry Forum Award
Second Place

Losing the Words

The words were once here.
They have flown miles away,
years into the future,
back into the mouths of many nights,
the woods, a deserted beach
where the tide takes days to come in,
dragging forbidden driftwood across the sand,
forgotten phrases from a place
where everyone we have loved
is dead. Whole sentences are buried
in furrowed earth, or on a beach
with broken shells like skulls.

To find the syllables again, read to me
the stories of the young,
for I can make them grow like
Rapunzel's hair, Pinocchio's nose,
or the goose that laid the golden egg
and hatches verbs, throws them
into an August night among the meteors
when nobody is watching.

Can anyone avoid the eventual solitude
of a street without language,
the deserted houses, the speechless windows?
The gibbous moon's hidden slice
is the word I've been searching for.
If you happen to see it, nail it
to the barn door, glue it
to the petal of the rose, taste it
in a ripe tomato, fold it into butterfly wings
that have long since forgotten
the cold coma of the cocoon.

Donna Pucciani
Wheaton, Illinois

Contest 19 ~ New York Poetry Forum Award

Third Place

How I Find the Words

I threw a stone into a dug well
At Grandma's homeplace.
Far down to bottom,
To water, and to resounding
Gurgle lapping against stone walls,
And I stood spellbound
As echoes vibrated
Along walls
Back to my ears.

Poetry in sound.

To find a word and continue
My poem, I thought
Of that well, how stone splashed,
Then gurgled.
I remember how it resonated
From side to side when I leaned
Over the opening and said
Silly words, high pitched,
Or in deepest bass
A boy of ten could.

Then it came to me.

In writing poetry, throw a word
Into the poem like a stone
Into that well.
There is a moment of waiting,
Listening, feeling, sensing,
Until it reaches bottom.
As it splashes emotions,
Inflection of voice rolls
Each word over an eager tongue.
A spiritual sense can listen
For proper echo. A warm sound
Caresses heart and soul
Imitating voice and well.

It resonates.

It is then I write on,
Closing the well,
Until I search
For another word.

Dennis Patton
Alexander, Arkansas

Contest 20 ~ Columbine Poets of Colorado Award
First Place

Private Brown
(Battle of Guadalcanal August 7, 1942 ~ February, 1943)

The war in nineteen forty-two
found me a soldier in the sand.
I fought a battle next to you.
We held our guns with steady hand.

The shells exploded all around.
We walked with death on foreign land
As shrapnel spread upon the ground,
we held our guns with steady hand.

The rain came down, the cruel sun beat
upon us as advancing band
was bravely faced on cautious feet.
We held our guns with steady hand.

You fought beside me day by day.
We trusted God would understand
when nightly as we knelt to pray,
we held our guns with steady hand.

One morning when the sun was high,
the price of death was war's demand.
I heard a blast and watched you die.
We held our guns with steady hand.

Sometimes I see you in the night,
relive the battle that we manned,
and volunteered our lives to fight
We held our guns with steady hand.

Shirley Elliott Cosby
Emory, Texas

Contest 20 ~ Columbine Poets of Colorado Award
Second Place

Dogwood Time

The day you left, the early dogwoods bloomed.
Though spring was showing furbelows and frills,
I knew that you were leaving to be groomed
for war. You'd learn the artistry and skills
of killing. Vowing you'd be back before
the dogwoods bloomed again, you said goodbye.
Avoiding any mention of the war,
you dried my tears and begged me not to cry.

Your letters came; I treasured every one
and answered back. I never missed a day.
There'd be a time when this old war was done;
all I could do till then was wait and pray.
The dogwoods bloomed again, their blossoms bright.
They brought no cheer, a melancholy sight.

And yet I hoped and planned for when we'd wed,
embroidered linen sheets and pillow slips
to place within the chest beside my bed,
while you were flying, fighting, bombing ships.
The battle of the Coral Sea took place;
I listened to the news till I was numb.
Your mama came to call—I saw her face
and knew the fateful telegram had come.

Each spring I watch the hummingbirds return
to sip the dogwoods' nectar. All alone
I wait to heal while trying to discern
a spark of life, my heart as dead as stone.
I shed my tears for what can never be,
for love we vowed beside the dogwood tree.

Joyce Shiver
Crystal River, Florida

Contest 20 ~ Columbine Poets of Colorado Award
Third Place

Surviving Bataan

Small silver sparkles of bombs arched down,
so numerous the explosions
caved in the sides of the trenches.
Then the enemy came at them from two sides,
too many … too many …
The troops retreated, much of their food
left behind. For three months they fought
on half-rations, mostly rice and canned tuna flakes,
but still held the front lines. They had
a month's respite when the enemy withdrew
to refit and reinforce—then hit them again
in waves, tidal waves of men,
leaving in their wake the flotsam
of blood and bodies.
To avoid annihilation, the sick
and enervated troops were ordered to surrender.

He thought he'd be afraid …
he could feel the hate oozing from his captors,
but he felt nothing, not even sadness.
They took his rifle, his helmet—
maybe they'd take his life.
It didn't matter. The could herd him
toward their slave camp, but
they weren't his Shepherd.
He raised a buddy, supported him
beneath the crook of his shoulder,
and began their march through hell.

Barbara Blanks
Garland, Texas

Contest 21 ~ Morton D. Prouty and Elsie S. Prouty Memorial Award
First Place

For the Man Who Hates Rocks
~ Translated by a rock hound

This poem is written by an agate.
You may think it impossible
for a stone to write a poem
but if you look at me closely
you will think it more impossible
for an agate to be. But I am.

Touch my now polished surface.
Read my delicate, deeply etched lines
that hint at my lifestyle,
my habits of loving, for eons
an earth that held me
in unspeakable passion.

But tension was my art
from the beginning. I pursued it
as if without choice
until I became at last
my own alchemist stone.
Touch me. I am magic.

I will teach you how to use
pressure with purpose, make you
possessor of valleys and mountains
never dreamed of, all-knower
of ancient secrets of living
and dying and loving uniquely.

I am earth's reverse rainbow, risen.
I have been found for a reason.
My eye cleared for seeing, I wait
for your eyes to engage mine of earth colors,
find trails into my intricate heart—
for inevitable love to begin.

Beryle Williams
Estes Park, Colorado

Contest 21 ~ Morton D. Prouty and Elsie S. Prouty Memorial Award

Second Place

Autumn in the Adirondacks

Within the forest silence greets my ears,
a gentle quietness—pine needle hush—
erasing all my raucous city fears,
far from the urban push and rush.

I hear a phoebe calling to its mate
somewhere in the branches high above my head.
The sunlight slants as afternoon grows late,
and leaves are stained glass hues—bright gold and red.

I'm walking in a glen of autumn brush,
with here and there the shadows made by stone.
And suddenly a snapped twig—cold chill rush!
How can this be? I thought I was alone!

Those tales of Sasquatch—wonder if they're true?
I strain my eyes—no creature comes in view.

My feet would like to run, but caught by thorn
I'm prisoner, my sweat pants won't let go.
I pull with all my might, the fabric's torn,
and now I move, but steps seem oh so slow.

Something is following and closing in,
I shiver in each fearful pulsing vein.
Imagination flies, and I begin
to feel sheer panic, breathlessness and pain.

I hide behind a pine tree, peeking out,
with perspiration streaming down my face.
I see two wild turkeys as they strut about,
oblivious of any human race.

And now I count the turkeys—there are **three**,
a fan-tailed cock, his loving mate—and **me**!

Ann Gasser
West Reading, Pennsylvania

Contest 21 ~ Morton D. Prouty and Elsie S. Prouty Memorial Award
Third Place

Two Weeks After the Vernal Equinox

The sun leaps over the prairie horizon
to hear the rhapsody of a returning meadowlark,
a rhapsody that lifts and warbles
through frost-scented air.

Khaki stalks of wheatgrass, buffalograss,
blue grama, and little bluestem, flattened
by heavy winter snows, show green
at the bunched bases.

Winter-thin prairie dogs scout the grass
around their burrows for tender shoots
as they prepare for spring mating
and the birthing of pups.

On toothpick legs, tiny burrowing owls
hunt for burrows that winter has emptied;
the freezing death of prairie dogs
supplies shelter for their chicks.

Antelope does, their bellies swelling
with twin fawns, search the prairie
for newly greened sage, false dandelion,
wild onion, and spreading daisies.

In sandy spaces between clumps
of grass, the hardy, six-pointed
sand lilies and delicate pink phlox
hug the ground with sudden beauty.

The meadowlark continues his rhapsodic
encouragement to arriving robins,
his ecstasy giving voice
to the promise of nature's renewal.

Art Elser
Denver, Colorado

Contest 22 ~ Poets Roundtable of Arkansas Award

First Place

Little Nighthawk Speaks

Mother told me Grandmother was
one of the flying women who searched
all night for the right place for home.
Each spring they cut and peeled saplings;
bent them into half moons to keep our lodge
strong as an embrace. Their shadows
over the wavering riverbank bent as well.

I thought our village in a horsehoe shape
a safe and warm place.
It was near the catttails and yellow flowers,
not far from rice stalks wading in the swamp.

Can you feel the spin of the earth in your hands?

Grandmother Blue Owl taught us to mark out
on our palms the rocks and meadows,
how light falls on the birch,
so we never failed to find home.

Does the inside of your hand teach you how to call them back?

I remember how heat poured over the babies,
waterfalling over the folded cliffs of their hearts
until their breath flew away to the moon.
I remember the red morning after, saplings blacken,
a cold wind, the silence; the deep silence.
Men asleep on the face of the stream,
women crumpled on village grounds
like big birds unable to fly.

There are many rumors of whole tribes
grown so small they flow away like winter ice.

We hidden children
watched the soldiers finally leave.
We held our wings in tight,
kept feet rooted in muddy reeds.

In late afternoon we walked to another life.
This spring night, after bending and shaping
new walls all day, we sit,
trace the lines of our palms
to help us tell Grandmother's stories.

Susan Stevens Chambers
Good Thunder, Minnesota

Contest 22 ~ Poets Roundtable of Arkansas Award

Second Place

Driving Down From Shiprock, New Mexico

Each clump of rabbit brush, it seems,
is tethered with a plastic grocery bag
that fills with wind and bobs with every gust.

Cottonwoods bathe their feet in the river
and melons swell in their sandy beds.
A horse nibbles alfalfa, swishing its tail.

Sparkling on the roadside are shattered bottles
and crystal of car windows
broken in the shrill, discordant night.

Junipers space themselves across the mesa,
Alike as pawns on a chessboard.
You can see where the precious rain has trickled.

Cliff graffiti splashed above the highway
Informs drivers that "Cowboys Rule"
and "Chucky loves Suzanne."

Little rocky roads bleed off into farms
Or up into the hills where derricks pull
From deep wells the oil to keep us moving on.

A sign recommends Whataburgers in Farmington.
Small cinderblock churches proclaim that Jesus Saves.
Every third vehicle is a pickup truck.

This is a homeland. It is hot and dry, but beautiful.
It is cheap and loud, but beautiful.
It is spicy and bad for you, but delicious.

You can follow dust devils across stark flats.
You can smell sagebrush underfoot.
Driving down from Shiprock, you can fall in love.

Joyce Kohler
Midway, Utah

Contest 22 ~ Poets Roundtable of Arkansas Award
Third Place

The Mooncalf

She strains
to keep pace with him,
his long legs striding ahead,
as she shuffles along the sidewalk,
always close,
always just out of reach.
Still she prays for his safety;
her heart skips a beat
at crossings,
worrying that he might
stumble and fall
on a curb,
or catch his toe
on the root-cracked walk,
and, eyes wide with terror,
come running back
scraped, scratched, bleeding,
hands held out before him
seeking Mother's touch.
It's always been this way,
but now
she dreads
his uncertain future.
Soon he'll have
no one to run to—
her hands are
twisted and swollen;
she struggles
to feed and to clean him,
to dress and comfort him,
to brush his graying hair.

Jim Barton
Huttig, Arkansas

Contest 23 ~ CSPS James E. MacWhinney Memorial Award
First Place

More Than a Half-Life* Ago

Among our dolls we toyed with growing up,
or torn old curtains veiled our princess heads.
Adept at plucking jumbled jacks or sticks,
we sprawled along the landing's stairs. The pair
of us would beg to swim late afternoons
then drag home, red and wrapped in soaking towels.
We seemed half sisters—not half cousins, no,
but like half sisters that our mothers were.

In summer's brand new Keds, yours red, mine blue,
school still in session on the front porch steps,
we scooted up a grade, slipped down, or skipped.
With books clutched in our arms, we hiked the mile
to bright library shelves and hurried home
to blankets in the grass or under trees
where side by side we shook our shoes and read.

Late Friday nights we watched the boxers jab
then switched to Paar—precocious as we were.
Smart talk collapsed to giggling while we lay
in gliders on the upstairs porch among
the maple limbs and leaves. There fireflies sparked
and cool midsummer breezes waved our hair
until the morning strained through bars of rain
that struck the guttered roof and beat the leaves.

Our maple tree is felled, the porches sold.
Our deserts stretch on two sides of the globe
where words between us failed, more rare than rain.
But any smell of rain transports me back
among our childhood limbs and leaves because
there you are still alive, and we are full
of unconcern for where our lives will lead—
half sisters more than half a life ago.

Barbara J. Funke
St. George, Utah

* *half-life: the time required for half of something to undergo a process, say, of deterioration*

Contest 23 ~ CSPS James E. MacWhinney Memorial Award
Second Place

Night in Monterey

Releasing darkness from their wings, the crows
appear on cue and cross the sky. Their caws
move west from inland trees to mouth of bay.
The sun, once proud distraction, loses light
below a shift of waves and misty hues
of gold and red. I love these migrant crows
that murder day. No longer blind to sound
I hear the night, how water knows its way,
rebukes cold cliffs as hollow cries from gulls
defy the wind. Between each cuff of waves
a silence bold as death takes time to know
itself. The sea holds back. The tern is still.
The crows drop down on trees. A thousand eyes
and muted caws attend this brittle peace.

Maurine Haltiner
Salt Lake City, Utah

Contest 23 ~ CSPS James E. MacWhinney Memorial Award
Third Place

A Rose Is a Rose

A rose climbs shy across the fence. It's not
my rose. It is a neighbor's rose but not
this family's, whose daughter was my son's
first love—he was four and she was three.
She'd drop her tiny underpants and run
the length of Ithaca as fiercely sweet
as any sprouting bean. Boldest atop
the linden tree, a tiny bird astride
the thinnest branches, coaxed my timid son
to venture further, consoled him if
he wouldn't. But these were not the ones
who planted awkward roses, climbing spare
and white as ghosts across our sagging fence,
perhaps the ones before—the old curmudgeon
who saved his trash in plastic sacks beneath
our bedroom window. Sad suburban
refuse spiced our summer dreams until
the ancient woody groaned with steaming waste
and nosed toward the city dump. It could
have been that stinginess that planted such
a rose, lanky bewilderment of thorns
so like a gawky, bony teen athwart
the wooden pickets, slouching mutely pale
as morning moons adrift in busy skies.
But still the name, "a rose" drips gorgeousness
across the page, and scent whose memory
can buckle knees and promise coolness still
to lonely cheeks. This rose that climbs amazed
across the fence, a harlequin of petals,
this rose refusing not to bloom persists
in calling up the rosiness of roses.

Claudia Van Gerven
Boulder, Colorado

Contest 24 ~ Ohio Award
First Place

Inside Another China of My Mind

These sticks must have fallen
from the sky. Strange things,
like the useless legs of some ancient
bird, lifting off for the last time.

Plant them in your bowl. Your fist
is the bird now, with no memory
of the use of its legs.
                                        Desperately
you try to land.

You poke at your food, tweeze
the rice in your bowl as you stand
unnaturally, unsteady, legless
in the marshland of your spoon
and fork mind.

Given nothing but these sticks, you stab
and shovel in blessed enmity, you pique
your way like a motherless bird on artless
legs through the stingy
heart of China.

Robert La Fleur
Ponsford, Minnesota

Contest 24 ~ Ohio Award

Second Place

Hansel and Gretel

This is the old forest where the children died.
Here is where their bones lie,
loose and white among the ashes,

tossed out as a matter of course,
like dirty dishwater or apple cores
thrown to the hogs.

Over there is a stand of aspen trees.
So young, so yellow, a trunk
for every bone, safe, too green to burn.

See how they bend on the hillside
beside the family cow, determined
to change the ending of the story.

Janice L. Freytag
Souderton, Pennsylvania

Contest 24 ~ Ohio Award
Third Place

Sleeping Dogs

Undisturbed,
sun upon our mangy fur,
we dream the dreams
of demons.

I have fed them,
allowed them in my house,
run with them in dark woods,
befriended the crippled ones.

When I am tired of this life,
as I often am,
they awaken with yawns of indifference,
ready to eat
at the table of my decaying flesh.

I invite them,
sit with them,
savor the taste of my own misgivings
at what happens to those
who try to do good.

Then I remember at once,
I am not good:
no one is.

My filthy rags
are the capes for these dogs,
for my dark days,
my doubt.

To question *is* to doubt;
to wonder, "Why me?"
is like asking, "Why is there blue
among the rainbow?"

A combination of all,
the absence of which is white,
nothingness.

All us sleeping ones
lie at the foot of that color wheel,
a pot of gold,
an awaited thing,
slumbering in a bliss undeserved,
given to saints and dogs alike.

Betty Leake
West Chester, Ohio

Contest 25 ~ Humorous Poetry Award
First Place

Emergency Poems

Because I date men who are literate, vain,
and easily flattered, I've found
they like to pretend they're the muse to my pen,
so I like to keep poems around.

There's one that is passionate, one that is sweet,
and several that end with a sigh,
and one fairly obscure (but with images pure)
for the poetry-editor guy.

At dinner, in bed, verses run through my head
depending on whom I'm impressing;
if he's sexy as hell, I'll whip out a rondel
before he has finished undressing.

Cool little haikus are stashed in the fridge,
the sonnets I keep in a drawer.
Rhyme and rhythm uncover the best in a lover—
and what else is poetry for?

Susan Whitley Peters
Lenexa, Kansas

Contest 25 ~ Humorous Poetry Award
Second Place

Stopping By E-Z Serve on a Sultry Evening

(With apologies to Robert Frost)

Whose store this is I think I know.
It's Bin Assad or Kim Chung Ho.
I did not plan on stopping here
But gas was cheap and I was low.

My little car must think it queer
To stop without a Rouse's near,
Between a bar and vacant lot,
With tattooed riffraff gulping beer.

How can they sell washtubs of Coke
For fifty cents and not go broke?
And Camel Lights are not too high
For hacking vagrant reeking smoke.

The store is packed and lottos beep,
But I have appearances to keep
And lines so slow they barely creep,
And lines so slow they barely creep.

Tommy Little
Pearl, Mississippi

Contest 25 ~ Humorous Poetry Award
Third Place

Time Conversion

Our friend, a Presbyterian,
just changed her church last week.
She's now an ardent Methodist
for reasons most unique.

It wasn't for theology,
for dogmas or for creed,
nor any articles of faith
or Scriptures one must heed.

Did not relate to offerings
or strictness of demands,
was not concerned with hymns or prayers,
or laying on of hands.

Her change did not pertain to grace
or ways to get to heaven … just
the old church met at half past ten,
the new one at eleven!

David L. Byrn
Prescott, Arizona

Contest 26 ~ Our American Indian Heritage Award

First Place

Wacipi

In the dry North Dakota heat,
they lean on the fence,
drinking Fanta and watching
the swaying, the shuffling,
the back and forth,
the elaborate dance, colored by
traditional dress,
the singers' chanting
the beat of the earth.
Everything converges—

feathers, drums, voices.
Pow, pow, pow.
Air, earth, dust, heat.
Pow, pow, pow.
Dancers luminescent, their sweat
clinging to skin as dark
in August as dirt.
And underneath the stomping feet
of the dancers, the fence being
leaned upon, the chairs
for the elders, the blankets
where families sit,
even the dirt can feel itself
mixing in and twirling about
with the living and the now
and the dead and the past.
Pow, pow, pow.

Mary Christine Delea
Oregon City, Oregon

Contest 26 ~ Our American Indian Heritage Award
Second Place

Due North

My father, one quarter Mohawk,
insisted his bed should face North or South,
that to sleep East to West
would cut his luck.

Charles Dickens slept facing north—
sure it inspired his writing.
His pillow memorized
the press of his silhouette,
one eye dreaming northward,
the compass point of his nose,
the currents and wrinkles of one sleeping cheek.

The Mohawk called what came from the north
the long human being, believed
the spirit of rivers lived in that place,
roiling with fish,
scales brimmed with visions,
gills charged with breath.

Colette Tennant
Salem, Oregon

Contest 26 ~ Our American Indian Heritage Award
Third Place

Searching Souls

You seek spirits in the stones,
search the sky for signs,
wait for an eagle to speak to you.
I whisper prayers in a sanctuary,
sing psalms, light candles,
wait for a statue to bleed.

You huddle damp and cramped
in a willow sweat lodge,
welcome the unseen.
I kneel in a tiny dark room,
hush my sins into silence,
welcome relief.

You purchase land and talk
of your homes made of tires and cans.
I place countless envelopes
into countless baskets and hear
of water purifiers for Rwanda.

We have grown so different over the years
yet close, maybe never closer.
Being Catholic was always part of being us.
We celebrate the seasons
gifting each other,
you, for me, to the Sisters of the White Plain,
me, for you, to the St. Jude's Children's Hospital.

You search, covering causes, covering continents.
I search closer to home,
my search not as worldly.
Years from now,
when we leave these bodies
and soar to our respective spirits,
we will be pleased
to reach the same space.

Coleen T. Ward
Melbourne, Florida

Contest 27 ~ Minute Award
First Place

The Shroud of Turin

The wispy image on a cloud
of linen shroud
may be a trace
of Holy face.
The Man it wrapped was crucified,
and blood had dried
from cutting rips
of cattail whips.
When unbelievers scoff, I grieve,
for I believe
it wrapped and spiced
my Jesus Christ.

Kitty Yeager
Arkadelphia, Arkansas

Contest 27 ~ Minute Award
Second Place

Desert Evening

The air is soft as gosling down
beneath the crown
of quiet stars.
Thirteen guitars
begin to strum a lazy theme—
a summer dream.
Two lovers meet
on darkened street.
Above the distant sandy dune
a shimmer moon
expands the night
with magic light.

Vera Ogden Bakker
West Bountiful, Utah

Contest 27 ~ Minute Award
Third Place

I Have the Audience Eating Out of My Hand

The chickens gather in the pen
and wonder when
they'll get their grain.
They wait in vain,

for first, I'll read them poetry.
the hens, to me,
are audience
inside the fence.

Then when my recitation's o'er,
they cluck, "No more!"
I pay them heed
and throw their feed.

Jim Barton
Huttig, Arkansas

Contest 28 ~ Missouri State Poetry Society Award
First Place

Rain

plays
a game of jacks,

splashing
city streets.

It captures
the rubber and metal

of passing cars,
then bounces on.

Pat Underwood
Colfax, Iowa

Contest 28 Missouri State Poetry Society Award
Second Place

New Christmas Toy

Load game
Take up mouse
Begin knightly quest
Endless tunnels and doors
Slay giant rat
Find gold
Bleed a little
Rest till healed
Endless tunnels and doors
Slay giant bat
Find sword
Hurl ball of fire
Overcome
Endless tunnels and floors
Check out map
Slay thief
Don magic shield
Save game
Back for more
Endless tunnels and stairs
Slay a dwarf
Slay a bear
Bleed some more
Replenish magic
Find gold
Save game
Load game
Endless tunnels and more

Edith Baker
Bountiful, Utah

Contest 28 ~ Missouri State Poetry Society Award
Third Place

Top Spinning Through Dry Leaves

I have spun this top before
    watched the swift circling
        the slow careening
        the tipsy wobble
    the collapse.

I do not need to spin this top again.
Open the drawer and put it back.

Claire van Breemen Downes
St. Cloud, Minnesota

Contest 29 ~ Louisiana State Poetry Society Award
First Place

Without Bells

He sits in a tomb of classroom,
silent as the childless desks,
and sees in this final hour of his life's work
what he leaves.
The day he dreamed has come,
and he wonders about tomorrows
where hours are not rung to life,
where silence in unbroken and
he can no longer measure
triumphs one period at a time.
He is accustomed
to a day's beginnings, endings,
time in fragments.
How will he exist without this perfect structure,
the flawless ringing that walled his words,
that brought the steady flow of faces?
The room grows shadowed in dusk
and from the hall I call him back to *this* day
and all yet to be.
We walk the journey from this life into the new,
his eyes rising from confinement
to the doors he has never
opened.

Budd Powell Mahan
Dallas, Texas

Contest 29 ~ Louisiana State Poetry Society Award
Second Place

To A Fisherman Soon To Marry

May your wedded life
be even better
than the best days
you can imagine on the lake

beginning
like anticipation at breakfast,
settling in to jobs and home
like choosing the place and lure,
overcoming problems
like snags that are bound to happen;

a mid-life pleasant
as warm breeze on your back,
togetherness
like loons, side by side,
co-operation
as one holds the net
while the other reels in,
harmony
like birdsong,
prosperity
like a full stringer;

senior years
tranquil as sun setting
beyond pines on far shore.

Shirley Ensrud
Blue Earth, Minnesota

Contest 29 ~ Louisiana State Poetry Society Award
Third Place

Just the wok, please
For Lewis Carroll

'Twas a brisket on the gas-powered stoves
Did baste and boil in flambé
All infused were a bag of cloves
And the mousse grazed spinach soufflé.

"Beware the white-starched chef, my son!
The jaws that bite, the hands that whisk!
Beware the boneless bird, and shun
Crustaceans served in bisque!"

He took his garlic press in hand:
Long time the caviar he sought
so rested he with his white Chablis
In a bed of penne from a pot.

And on simmer the gravy stood,
The white-starched chef with eyes of flame,
Dredged the roux into ragout,
To bubble at his refrain:

"One egg! Now two! Beat through and through
An omelet for a midnight snack!"
Each thyme he sizzled with Julienne,
Sweat dripping down his back.

And hast thou seen the white-starched chef?
Brie in his arms, the sauce of soy,
"Oh stir-fry day, Scallions! Sauté!"
He chortled in his joy.

'Twas a brisket on the gas-powered stoves
Did baste and boil in flambé
All infused were a bag of cloves
And the mousse grazed spinach soufflé

Julie Nelson
Orem, Utah

Contest 30 ~ Barbara Stevens Memorial Award

First Place

The Lie I Do Not Tell

There is a lie I do not tell,
a child conceived but not born.

Some say it does not count.
But it still feels like death,
taking up space in the underground,

crowding out the forsythia
that never asked anything of me
but two weeks of honesty in April.

Janice L. Freytag
Souderton, Pennsylvania

Contest 30 ~ Barbara Stevens Memorial Award
Second Place

To Junior

You swam in the cup of water our cousin Donn
said a person could drown in. You were the liquid
spotting Grandmother's pillow, Uncle Norman's towel
that would not dry, the soundless wet circle
always on the dining room table.

You schooled me in fear of swimming holes, lakes,
rivers, waves. When Mother took me to the city pool,
you dived from Donn's cup, tried to pull me under.

Relinquish your power over me, Junior. I can no longer
live in the shadow of your swollen young body.

Wilda Morris
Bolingbrook, Illinois

Contest 30 ~ Barbara Stevens Memorial Award
Third Place

Fingerprints

Children with eyes the color of his
ran through the hallways of my days.
Their shrieks and laughter linger
in my naptime non-sleep.
If I'd never washed away
those fingerprints on the hallway walls,
I could now follow
their smudged stickiness
back to the days of him
and our children's noise
and Kool-Aid spilling
from plastic tumblers.

Janet Watson
Wesley Chapel, Florida

Contest 31 ~ Dorman John Grace Memorial Award

First Place

Snakeskin Boots

In scruffy snakeskin boots at traffic stop,
A man with sign was begging food today.
Delayed by signals on my way to shop,
His window-knocking blew my joy away.
Behind a brush of copper-colored beard,
I saw a college friend with law degree,
But all his Irish charm had disappeared
And drugs had iced the eyes of tropic sea.
My imitation leather purse was thin,
With just enough for jeans and gasoline,
Yet passing by this Brother seemed a sin,
So mercy won as lights were turning green.
  As drivers honked, I mourned his wasted years,
  Then drove away before he saw my tears.

Kitty Yeager
Arkadelphia, Arkansas

Contest 31 ~ Dorman John Grace Memorial Award
Second Place

Blind Trust

"In human relations kindness and lies are worth a thousand truths."
~ Graham Greene

He never would admit that she was gone,
though he'd not seen her face in twenty years.
Dear Cora was his sight—his strong piton
who kept him safe from falling, calmed his fears,

and made the days of darkness he endured
more bearable, for she was always there
to serve his meals, to keep him reassured,
to shave his beard, and lead him to his chair.

For more than sixty years, his loving mate
had served him well and listened to each gripe.
Without complaint, she did not hesitate
to heed his contant call of: *"Light my pipe."*

Now eldest daughter Mary tends the blind,
and he's content—she's *Cora* in his mind.

Valerie Martin Bailey
San Antonio, Texas

Contest 31 ~ Dorman John Grace Memorial Award

Third Place

Fishing Expedition

Your grizzled cheek says, *Here I am, come back*
from days of fishing with the guys. Your smile
says, *It feels good to be here.* You unpack
by dumping gear then hold me for a while.
The water in the shower runs. You sing
a scale, emerge smooth-shaven, slick as fish
you caught and freed, regretful not to bring
me fish for dinner. But you share a wish
I'd join you, say I'd like it if I tried.
For each of us, I pour a glass of wine
that nets your stories, hours of humor, pride.
We toast your safe return. I reel my line,
    my ear the hook, the bait this pool of peace
    until you're off again: catch and release.

Barbara J. Funke
St. George, Utah

Contest 32 ~ Poetry Society of Oklahoma Award
First Place

Primavera

Primavera, ha! Spring comes seeming again with the same old tart renewal, always like always, over and ever over, repeating the need to start something, some new triteness, a new batch of wet business, a flood of mud, fickle sun and green teases. Flaunting its crocuses. Tricking us into putting away mittens a month too early. Waiting for songbirds, having to make do with starlings. Waiting through the cold rain, the last ice storm of the season, then more cold rain, and ditches and streams and rivers running out of their banks, making the whole state it sometimes seems one big lake. And fog. And dead animals out from under the snow cover, and dead skunks again along the highway, their final effusions hanging in the chill night air like incense burned to some disgusting god of garbage. *Lasciate ogni speranza, voi ch'entrate.** Backyards covered with twigs to pick up. And more of those damned crocuses, trying to make us think of Spring's pretty reputation, as though we are living in a greeting-card world. The wonder is not that the crocuses are here again, but that they prompt the same old sentiments year after year. And after them the daffodils. The price of daffodils, ultimately, is the same as the price of sump pumps. April showers bring April's misery, and May flowers may or may not flower. Spring's vaunted profusion will string us along two months yet until everything's properly green, as advertised. *Traditore! Serpente!* The best that can be said of it's that Winter's finally done. Probably. *Va fan culo!***

John Calvin Rezmerski
Mankato, Minnesota

* *"Abandon all hope, ye who enter here" ~ Dante*
** *"Up yours! ~ numberless Italians*

Contest 32 ~ Poetry Society of Oklahoma Award
Second Place

Spring: Magnificent in Second Place

If I compared an April day to you,
My Love, no hyacinth, no twilight skies,
no nest of robin eggs, no springtime blue
could match the azure color of your eyes.

Blossoms of peach and apples blemish trees
when set against the pink tones of your skin.
Sun glints on water thrill until one sees
that, in a match, your golden hair would win.

Kittens curled in sleep form gentle lines,
but not as fine as curves that sketch your face.
Need I say more? Your beauty undermines
seasonal splendor in this unfair race.

Since April fades compared to your fair form,
I will not use your measure as a norm.

Rose Ann Spaith
Columbus, Ohio

Contest 32 ~ Poetry Society of Oklahoma Award
Third Place

Spring Cleaning

Before my neighbor and I could boil eggs,
she to dye for egg hunts,
and I to symbolize life at my Passover Seder,
we burrowed into our homes with brush and broom,
invading closets and infiltrating cupboards
with cleansers and alien chemicals,
tossing the jetsam of winter
into plastic twist-tie bags.
It was as though God, who spent His time
setting bridal gowns on dogwoods
and igniting azalea bushes,
needed our help to renew the world.
We did not see each other for a week.
Then, eager to show off her accomplishments,
she enticed me at our fence:
"At my house, I just made fresh coffee."
"At my house," I responded,
"I just baked a pie."

Russell H. Strauss
Memphis, Tennessee

Contest 33 ~ Save Our Earth Award
First Place

The River's Edge

I walk down to the river's edge
looking for its resounding hymn
as water slips over rusty stones.

Spring walks in other places
spoke in snow-diamond parables,
long hours of life behind me.

Mud tugs at my boots, thoughts pile.
Everything does what it must do—
starlings gather on budding olive trees,

magpies squawk into frightened flight,
ducks drift down creek with the north wind.
In clarity of greening open fields

And river flowing to the lake,
I know, no matter where I step
In a world of thistles and weeds,

I do what I must do.
My head comes up, back straightens
When I walk the river's edge.

Beverly Cook
Sandy, Utah

Contest 33 ~ Save Our Earth Award
Second Place

Legacy

Across a wintry backdrop filled with prophecies of snow,
a skein of sandhill cranes uncoils on the way toward rest.
Russet flickers under wings from the reflected glow
of flame-to-ember sunset banked against the west.

Earth's oldest bird, now sailing thermals over sage and sand,
once soared above savannahs that stretched to cooling seas.
Pterodactyl echoes sound from this primeval band;
wings of feather once were leather on the buoyant breeze.

These elders of the airways flew in ages-old migration
when man was but a fledgling, and the world was wrapped in cold.
Now, humans are a factor in a delicate equation,
and if we keep the balance is a tale yet to be told.

As habitat diminishes to satisfy our greed,
where will these ancient majesties find space to rest and feed?

Shirley Balance Blackwell
Los Lunas, New Mexico

Contest 33 ~ Save Our Earth Award
Third Place

Envy

Those connected to the earth
arise in the morning shivering glad
as prairie grass, feeling their roots
beneath feet, floor and soil.
The pines shelter them with dark-raised arms,
chanting the mantras of the forest.

For these children of the land,
everything is silence
and green, or else the rocky
pink emptiness of the desert,
the safety of mountains.
they go hiking and never get lost,
never fear mountain lions
or the grizzly loping near the river
who suddenly looks up.

While they are touching the rain
with the tips of their tongues,
or tracking puma,
I am a strap-hanger on the subway
whose backpack carries books.
not protein and water. My woods
are the crowds hurrying nowhere,
my provinces tall buildings
with only a strip of sky between.

Donna Pucciani
Wheaton, Illinois

Contest 34 ~ Ben Lomond Poets Award
First Place

Holding the World

But there is no dollar value on hope.
~ a lawyer

We are the rich ones, the millionaires.
We are not the mountain or the ones
climbing—but the treasures inside
every mountain, the ore long buried
in sand castles along the coast of Spain.
We have shining jewels for eyes.

We are rich like the whirl of evening sky
that shines on an old blue farmhouse,
like hopes hanging from a clothesline,
sheets billowing in icy wind, like
all the secret upspent bills that hide
in a forgotten lady's purse, like her
trembling lips that resemble roses just
kissed by morning dew—that rich.

We are the anticipation that is free
and fully blessed. We are the angels
who hear and respond to our own
longing, the fancy messengers who
call us in the night. We are the ones
naming and the things we name. We
hold the world in our bankrupt hearts.

Margo LaGattuta
Rochester, Michigan

Contest 34 ~ Ben Lomond Poets Award
Second Place

A Lover's View from Upper Deck

My eyes began to revel and explore
The day our ship surveyed Alaska's shore.
I watched the mountains rise up from the sea
Like great stone fountains in a jagged spree.
A cape of snow enveloped each tall peak
Like white brassieres upon a fine physique,
Revealing how the Tetons got their name
From lonely Frenchmen viewing them the same
As body parts evoking home and frock,
And not just monoliths of frigid rock.

A need began to grow inside my chest
As though my heart was stranded on some crest
As cold as death and sharp as any knife.
I scanned the mountainsides for signs of life,
But I saw none upon those ancient spires,
No creatures capable of life's desires,
Just awesome beauty, awful vacancy,
And nothing there to warm and nourish me.
Before the sun could set and night embark
Upon its aims to make the mountains dark,
I turned and left the deck to look for her,
A thermal charm that men like me prefer.

Larry Hand
Woodstock, Georgia

Contest 34 ~ Ben Lomond Poets Award
Third Place

Norwegian Cliffs

I don't know how I got here
but I am. Too high to see
forever, too afraid to look
down, I lie prostrate
upon the granite ledge flattened
so as not to rend the sky.

Monolithic cliffs, too old
to remember their age, drop
their sheer faces to a bottom
somewhere below the limits
of vision, somewhere beyond
the source of gravity. Its force
slides me face first toward
the edge while fear clenches
my ankles.

All is headstone gray.
A haunting Nordic folk strain mourns
its way through crevice walls.
I can only listen as the slab
beneath presses me
against the cobalt sky.

Too high to see forever,
too afraid to look down.
I don't know how I got here
but I am.

Tommy Little
Pearl, Mississippi

Contest 35 ~ Massachusetts State Poetry Society
First Place

Kyrielle to My Husband

They've had their drinks of water for the night.
I've read them books. I've kissed their foreheads, too.
Blankets are tucked; they're shadowed in nightlight.
I want to share a glass of wine with you.

Tie up the weight of life into a sack.
Tonight, there's nothing that you need to do.
Warm waters fill the tub where we'll lie back.
I want to share a glass of wine with you.

I'll light the candles. You slip off your clothes.
Let me untie the laces of your shoes.
the bath is scented heavily with rose.
I want to share a glass of wine with you.

The air carries the sounds of violins.
I'll wash your hair with honey-sweet shampoo.
I've warmed oils to massage into your skin.
I want to share a glass of wine with you.

With sponges, loofahs, soaps of different size,
I'll scrub your body. You relax, renew.
Immerse yourself, come, sit between my thighs.
I want to share a glass of wine with you.

Our lives return to normal with the sun,
and time will not stand still for us to do
the little things that we have always done.
I want to share a glass of wine with you.

Coleen T. Ward
Melbourne, Florida

Contest 35 ~ Massachusetts State Poetry Society
Second Place

Eden All Over Again

One morning Adam walks out the front door
to pick up the morning paper, confronting
a nine-foot long Burmese python spread across
the front porch, waiting, he thought, for Checkers,
the black-and-white Irish setter still sleeping on his
down-filled pillow in the hall. What to do, he thought,
before deciding he must inform his wife, Eve.
"You'll never believe what's on the front porch!
Not in a billion years!"
"Be serious," she murmurs and rolls over,
suggesting he let her sleep a few minutes more.
"No! Come and see, but close the door in the hall."
Eve crawls out of bed and follows, giving little thought
at this early hour to Adam's obvious excitement.

He cracks open the door and points at the monster
still spreading its long length but now a little closer.
"Oh, my God!" Eve shrieks, "Where did it come from?"
"From somebody's basement probably; people do that,
you know, when they get too big."
"For goodness sake, call 911 and tell them to be quick!"
Adam dials and explains the situation.
"No, I've not been drinking! Come immediately
before it slithers away."

They wait inside, looking through the curtains, anxious
when Checkers joins them. The dog knows without seeing
that something is awry. He barks, clawing at the door,
wanting out to tackle the monster that waits to tackle him.
The newsboy passes, throws the paper, drives away.
The snake is not intimidated and remains motionless,
seemingly to wait, if necessary, for a millennium.

So engrossed, they jump when the phone rings.
Adam answers, listens in disbelief, hangs up, then explains:
"They say if the owner doesn't come to claim it, it will be picked up
and taken to the zoo; said to call back later."

Hungry now, they go to the kitchen; Eve makes coffee
with apologies for being without eggs, cereal or milk.
"How about a piece of last night's apple pie?"
"Sounds good," Adam says, continuing to complain
about the inefficiencies of public offices and waste of tax dollars.

Jeanine Mah
Memphis, Tennessee

Contest 35 ~ Massachusetts State Poetry Society
Third Place

Greetings to an Uzbekistan Torturer

How're you today? Fine?
A good mood and good health
seem like signs of good fortune
for a life well lived.
Don't you feel that?
In passing, though, Takir Nurmukhamedov
was not fortunate, given his death
at your hands, those of a
government employee with a family to care for, I guess.
Do your children have career day at school in Andijan?
Do they ask what you do?
"*Come to school with us, Dad. We're*
so proud of you.
What do you do? Can you show our teacher
what you do?
Do they worry about your smoking, your health?
You don't have to smoke at home. No one
to burn, no flesh to singe. And smoking
is bad for your health. Cancer, you know.
Lungs don't grow back like fingernails.
Stability is everyting, when governing a dictatorship.
Continuing control is imperative as
finding out the truth about protestors
who demand to stand in front of soldiers
with their entire families until they're killed,
hundreds on the unluckiest thirteenth of May.
They got what they asked for—
liberation by death,
like Takir received from you
after burns and beatings to questions
about names of nonexistent outside agitators.
But you're doing your job,
keeping your world safe for your children,
who don't know what their father does,
but will someday.

Don't worry about us judging you.
We can't find your city on a map
or pronounce your name properly,
probably.
Do you remember your name?

Rosemary Dunn Moehler
St. Lawrence, South Dakota

Contest 36 ~ Poetry Society of Tennessee Award
First Place

A Twist of a Dream

In my bed I slant toward you.
I am falling into you at night.
This mattress in my father's house
unites us in a twist of a dream.

I am falling into you at night.
I enter your breathing, and your heart
unites us in a twist of a dream.
We both float above ourselves.

I enter your breathing, and your heart
whispers words we can't remember.
We both float above ourselves,
become diaphanous as we kiss,

whisper words we can't remember.
This mattress in my father's house
becomes diaphanous as we kiss.
In my bed I slant toward you.

Margo LaGattuta
Rochester, Michigan

Contest 36~ Poetry Society of Tennessee Award
Second Place

Harriet Travels Alone

She heard the threads' voices
as she traced the stitched map,
made easy her choices—
Ol' Ma's quilt on her lap.

As she traced the stitched map
hidden secrets she read.
Ol' Ma's quilt on her lap
patterned fabric and thread.

Hidden secret she read
the quilt held a story,
pattered fabric and thread
patchworked freedom's glory.

The quilt held a story
soft-told symbols and signs,
patchworked freedom's glory
her path handsewn in lines.

Soft-told symbols and signs
made easy her choices—
her path handsewn in lines.
She heard the thread's voices.

Coleen T. Ward
Melbourne, Florida

Contest 36 ~ Poetry Society of Tennessee Award
Third Place

Pantoum from a Broken Moon

The sirens scream with lights of red and blue.
It is my fault since he is always right
I don't know what I am supposed to do.
I can't find the moon but he holds me tight.

It is my fault since he is always right
I live within locked doors and windows too.
I can't find the moon but he holds me tight.
He says he loves me so it must be true.

I live within locked doors and windows too.
I took the knife to cut holes in the night—
He says he loves me so it must be true.
Do I run now or should I stay and fight?

I took the knife to cut holes in the night—
I don't do what I'm supposed to do.
Do I run now or should I stay and fight?
The sirens scream with lights of red and blue.

Frances Brinkley Cowden
Cordova, Tennessee

Contest 37 ~ Poetry Society of Michigan Award

First Place

Mama

I dreamed of you last night.
The moonlight may have brought
you here. It streamed through the window
and laid a silver spread upon the bed,
my marriage bed.

He slept beside me, satisfied, while
I wept in silence and prayed for sleep
that finally came.

You did not speak, but I could read
the message in your face: *This is the way*
it is; a woman marries, submits to a man,
bears his children, works hard,
does the best she can with what she has.

Oh, Mama, why must this be true?
I was just a girl, left to care for Papa
and the boys. I wanted to finish school,
not cook and clean and wash and iron
and listen to my brothers complain and curse.
After two years, I found escape, challenged
with a crumpled dollar bill when I declared
that for two bits I would marry just to get away.

Now here I am, right where you expected
me to be. But I have learned your lessons well.
After breakfast, I will clean the dusty windows
and invite the sunshine in.

Linda Banks
Mesquite, Texas

Contest 37 ~ Poetry Society of Michigan Award
Second Place

Such Mourning Songs

Your first hospital stay
brought so many flowers, balloons, and cards
that the wealth was shared with others,
no more or less deserving.
Then diagnosis and confirmation.
By your fifth hospitalization,
a few phone calls;
after your eighth visit,
we were on our own.
Six months of on our own
and six months of you, lying, dying, in the bed.
Six months of running, hurrying everywhere,
because I couldn't bear to think of you
alone,
and leaving you alone because
no one would stay with you.
Six months of the disease
biting, eating, finally devouring you.
The last day's last hours
swaddled you in sleep.
Raspy breathing echoed through the rooms.
Even in the bathroo,, running water, I could hear you.
There was no escape
and at the end I wanted one.
Your pain was my pain.
I held your hand when
I needed someone to hold mine.
It was Sandburg's fog
that came in on cats' paws,
and your death that came in on tigers' claws,
shredding my frazzled grasp on immortality.
But I sat holding your hand, reading you poetry,
page after page of poetry,
listening to your breathing.
Then I was holding you in my arms,
singing you Groce's "Bad, Bad Leroy Brown."
I don't know why.

I think it was because I knew the words to it.
Then, you were gone.

At your funeral,
hearing, but not listening to the offered condolences.
Until, "I know I should have called
or come by, but..."
and, "I've been so busy; I knew you would call
if you needed anything."
Six months of being alone with you and I was never alone.
Six hours of being with them and
I am more alone than I ever thought possible.

Coleen T. Ward
Melbourne, Florida

Contest 37 ~ Poetry Society of Michigan Award
Third Place

Fear of Flying

"...Turn but a stone, and start a wing."
~ Francis Thompson

Only the promise of seeing her husband,
away for nine months in Iraq, could have brought her
to the airport on this freezing December day.

Despite her anxiety about flying, and a scratchy throat,
she boarded the first of several connecting flights
to Milan, where he would meet her.

After a bumpy landing in Chicago in the midst
of a blizzard, she huddled, shivering, feverish,
in the terminal. All departures delayed.

A tall, silver-haired man waiting for the same flight
brought her bottled water and aspirin from the airport shop
then produced a soft, warm blanket from somewhere.

When they finally boarded the 747 to Frankfort,
he helped her to her seat, told the flight attendant
she was ill and needed assistance, then left.

By the time they landed, eight hours later, her fever
had broken. The tall man appeared, steered her
through customs and onto the Milan flight.

When she turned to thank him, he was gone,
leaving only a soft glow where he had been standing.
She would never be afraid to fly again.

Marilyn Stacy
Dallas, Texas

Contest 38 ~ Lighten Your Life Award
First Place

Plant Sale

When I went out this morning,
I spied a lot of males.
They were waiting to enter the gate
at one of my neighbors' plant sales.
But I couldn't understand
why there was such a line,
and what the draw could be,
until I caught a glimpse of the sign
that said, "Naked Ladies For Sale."*

Catherine L'Herisson
Garland, Texas

*Naked Lady is another
name for Spider Lilies

Contest 38 ~ Lighten Your Life Award

Second Place

The Postman Seldom Rings Twice

I love to browse through catalogues
for crystal cats and china dogs,
exotic spices from Bombay
or vases garbed in cloisonné.

Fresh salmon from Alaskan streams,
divinity and chocolate cremes;
I go online or telephone
and what I crave becomes my own.

The markets of the world display
their treasures for me every day—
to be delivered to my door.
How could I ask for any more?

But now and then things go awry,
a broken glass or thawed-out pie;
and that is when I must confess
I suffer Post Traumatic Stress!

Dian S. Barnett
Marietta, Georgia

Contest 38 ~ Lighten Your Life Award
Third Place

Hunger Pangs

Now at the risk of being rude
I'm writing about stale food:
The kids are gone, just me and him
but still the fridge fills to the brim

with lettuce, wilted, milk that's sour,
leftovers ranker by the hour.
Eggs, two dozen in a batch
become so old they almost hatch.

Bland or spicy, sour or sweet
There's nothing in there fit to eat.
Our appetites are healthy, though
So off to Sizzler we will go.

Martha P. Morrise
Roy, Utah

Contest 39 ~ Iowa Poetry Association Award
First Place

The Easter Egg Hunt
(a Samisen)

Grab your basket and start hunting—find the eggs—
Find the eggs!
For it's Easter and they're hiding—find the eggs.
There are yellow ones and pink ones,
Lots of striped ones and some plain.
But the clouds are building 'round us
And we hope it doesn't rain!
Find the eggs!

Fill your baskets to the brim now—find the eggs—
Find the eggs!
Just look everywhere around you—find the eggs.
Some are snuggled in the bushes.
Others perched up in a tree.
But those clouds are getting darker.
It might rain, we'll have to see.
Find the eggs!

Tiny raindrops hit my forehead—find the eggs—
Find the eggs!
We may have to run for cover—find the eggs.
If we hurry we might make it
Right before we all get wet.
Oh, it's only a light sprinkle.
There's no need to be upset.
Find the eggs!

Diane "Dee" Bowlin
Oklahoma City, Oklahoma

Contest 39 ~ Iowa Poetry Association Award
Second Place

Bright New Shoes

I've got new shoes, new bright red shoes!
Shoes to take me everywhere.
Shoes for dancing, shoes for prancing,
Shoes just perfect anywhere.
I've got new shoes, new bright red shoes!
Hear them tapping on the street!
Tap, tap, tapping, tap, tap, tapping,
Tapping to my dancing beat
Oh, tap, tap tappity, ta-tappity, tappity,
Tap, tap, tappity, tappity feet!
Neat!

Lee Barry Priete
Citrus Springs, Florida

Contest 39 ~ Iowa Poetry Association Award

Third Place

Smart Dog

I have a little dog
My daddy bought for me,
And he's the nicest dog
That any dog can be.

He's very smart, you know.
When he was just a pup,
He knew when I was sad
And tried to cheer me up.

He'd bark a little song
And then he'd start to prance.
Though Mom does not agree,
I think he tried to dance.

When I get up each day,
He gives a joyful yap,
Then crawls into my bed
So he can take a nap.

Esther Towns
Selma, Indiana

Contest 40 ~ New Jersey Poetry Society Award

First Place

Yoked

"And the two shall become one flesh."

We slip into the yoke
in those dandelion days.
Even as we learn
to walk the furrows
we step on each other's feet.

So little we understand
the confines of this span,
abrasions of shoulders,
concessions of gee and haw.

So little we understand
the length of dogged days
required to plw these fields,
to plant a crop.

I learn to slow my step
to match your steady gait,
for the essence of a yoke
lies in facing foward,
two joined in purpose,
until the lulling tempo
erases thoughts of 'me'
and all is 'we.'

Somewhere up ahead,
the unimaginable furrow
that must be plowed by one.

Doris Stengel
Brainerd, Minnesota

Contest 40 ~ New Jersey Poetry Society Award
Second Place

Prayer for Katherine

She stretches tiny hand for Sippy cup,
then round baby eyes begin to droop,
lids flutter dreamily as tiny tube
is inserted into her hand; she murmurs
soft sighs then whimpers as breathing
becomes heavy. I stroke the wet curls
as she is lifted from the crib, carried
lovingly by the gentle nurse down
marble halls to double doors; there
I release her to the team in white
and turn into my husband's arms.

Create in her a new heart, O God.

I sit silently in prayer, imagine her
there in the theater amid bright lights
where she is the star of the show,
17 pounds of soft baby flesh upon
stainless steel table and where four
gloved hands poise above her tiny
infant chest while surgeon's music
morphs sterile silence into serenity.

Even there your hand shall guide him.

Here in the family room, we wait,
newspapers unread, coffee half-drunk,
listening for the phone, for a door to open,
for our name to be called. He appears
in paper shoes, his tired eyes recognize us.
He nods as we stand and move toward him,
and then he smiles—a physician's triumph.

My heart leaps for joy, I will give thanks.

Barbara Lewie Berry
Mansfield, Texas

Contest 40 ~ New Jersey Poetry Society Award
Third Place

They Got It In the End

In camouflage and bright orange hat,
John sat still as could be,
to wait for a prize buck you'd think,
not so as you will see.

He married Kate for all her wealth,
to live life leisurely,
to drive nice cars and get the girls,
young ones, especially.

But things began to go awry,
and he began to think,
what if she died, I'd have it all,
then took another drink.

If Kate was lured out to the woods,
to check on me someday,
she might then be mistaken for
some other hunter's prey.

And here's the really funny part,
of how this came about,
"she" hired a man to do "him" in,
made sure no one found out.

They studied each and every move,
just how it should be done,
how John would sit in his tree-stand,
and buying the right gun.

They even measured out with scope,
the slug's trajectory,
she wanted to exact revenge,
for his debauchery.

That fateful day this all took place
    she kept a watchful eye,
from her secluded spot nearby,
    with full intent to spy.

They were all set, each in their spot,
    the fun would soon begin,
the shots rang out from far and wide,
    it made their heads all spin.

They are not sure how it transpired,
    newspaper headlines read,
the cops are still a bit confused,
    how they could "all" be dead.

Marilyn K. Smith
Fair Grove, Missouri

Contest 41 ~ Wyopoets Award
First Place

Raccoons Ate My Roof

I heard the gnawing on my house—
knew it was bigger than a mouse.
And sure enough, we found out soon
the chomping sounds were from a coon.

And not just one—a raccoon crew—
all chewing hard as they could chew.
I think they also used their claws
to augment damage from their jaws.

Down through the roof, those rascals came
and to *my* attic staked a claim.
Nocturnal beasts, they romped and played
until my nerves were badly frayed,

and rain was leaking through the roof.
Insurance men would need some proof,
and they would need to check my claim
to see if raccoons were to blame.

"Did you *see* coons?" the agent asked.
"I did," I said, "but they were masked."
He sighed and brought his clipboard out
to see what this was all about.

He came, he saw, he verified
that my complaint was justified.
A brand new roof would be installed,
but first those raccoons must be hauled

out to some rustic country place
where hollow trees, not attic space,
can be their homes and they'll do well,
and I won't live in "raccoon hell."

In *Have-a-Hearts*, nice humane traps,
the coons were caged mid snarls and snaps.
With cages in the pickup bed,
and snarling raccoons watered, fed,

we started out to find some land
where humans had not made a stand—
some untamed land with trees and brush,
beyond the sound of traffic rush.

We wondered how far we would drive
to find a place where they'd survive.
Sure, I was peeved at damage done,
but after all is said and done,

it's really not their fault, you know—
they simply have nowhere to go.
New houses fill their habitats,
and I'm just glad they weren't polecats.

Valerie Martin Bailey
San Antonio, Texas

Contest 41 ~ Wyopoets Award
Second Place

Dust to Dust ~ Spain's Andalusian Vultures
(Form: Ottava Rima)

The vulture sits his craggy spot and waits
until the sun-struck rocks are warm enough.
When thermal currents rise, he activates
a ten-foot spread of wing and leaves the bluff
behind. Still-rising sun illuminates
his sandy plumage, coffee-colored ruff.
He sits the air in silence like a king,
perusing all that dies beneath his wing.

Great staring eye with telescopic sight
can spot a tiny creature lying still.
He crosses and re-crosses from his height,
alert to smallest sign of life, until
two days at least have passed. His circling flight
descends for closer view. An ancient thrill
suffuses tip to tail. He takes his chance,
plants feet on land, begins his circling dance

around blue-bloated carcass of dead goat.
Irresolute in fear, he stands erect,
then swivels, stretching fully naked throat
to peck at corpse, observing the effect.
Exultantly he croaks one rasping note,
then throws his beak into the flank. Blood-specked,
he strips the hide from reeking, lifeless frame,
then penetrates the viscera. No shame

deters the famished feasting, joined by more
than twenty of his brothers from the sky.
A mule may last two hours, an oxen, four.
In half an hour, goat skeleton is dry.
Egyptian vultures fling in to explore
the leavings of the larger birds. They try
the skull, the joints, extract the spinal cord,
clip tendons, membranes, dodging through the horde

of stuffed and panting griffons in the sun.
Last comes the bearded vulture, lammergeier,
to seize the largest bones of skeleton
and smash them on the rocks. His heart's desire
is marrow. Nothing's left when he is done
but empty skull and bits which ants acquire.
Notorious birds are scavengers, reduce
Spain's reeking refuse, BUT—what's man's excuse?

Edith Baker
Bountiful, Utah

Contest 41 ~ Wyopoets Award
Third Place

Some Things Can't Be Explained

A wild crow showed up one day
and adopted my big brother Andrew.
Jack, the crow, never made a mess on our sidewalk
or porch, didn't peck at our tomato plants,
and chased other birds away from the garden,
so Mom and Dad didn't mind him being here.

That bird rode around on my brother's shoulder
every day, until Andrew left for the war
and asked me to take care of him.
Even when Jack few off with other crows,
he was always home by dark, until the day
we got word Andrew was missing in action.

Jack didn't come home. I thought he was dead.
But almost a year later that bird
flew into the yard and landed on my head,
like he hadn't been gone at all.
He was kind of wild and scraggly looking,
but it was Jack all right.

I ran hollering to tell Mom,
and not five minutes later an army car
pulled up with the best news we could ever hear.
Andrew was on his way home.
When he got there, he looked kind of wild
and scraggly too, but nobody cared.
Jack knew. I tell you, that crow is psychic.

Marilyn Stacy
Dallas, Texas

Contest 42 ~ Nebraska State Poetry Society Award
First Place

Asphyxiation

Weeks ago I shut a bee in the window,
afraid of getting stung in the dark.

On this warm fall day I open the glass,
find his body curled at the base of the screen.

Freedom must have sung to him for days,
a touch of honey
and home
on the wind.

Joshua Conklin
Oxford, Connecticut

Contest 42 ~ Nebraska State Poetry Society Award
Second Place

Occupant

This stranger, my body, seems for unknown
years to have inhabited
a distant corner of my mind,
like a quiet boarder given the spare room.
No raucous parties, no loud,
late-night noises,
no pungent smells of cooking to intrude
into the living room of ideas;
ignored, forgotten, tuned out
since those early days of tumult.
We speak briefly
during monthly routines of
maintenance and rent.
fulfilling mutual obligations.

After years of silent solitude, my tenant
comes knocking on the screen door,
demanding to be welcomed in.
Out of context, and at an odd
hour of the night, what should be
a familiar face
is hard to place. I'm told
this neighbor has family,
all of whom watch
each others' backs.

Shirley Balance Blackwell
Los Lunas, New Mexico

Contest 42 ~ Nebraska State Poetry Society Award
Third Place

Ungrounded Facts

The ground is unpredictable.

Speak to those in San Francisco
and other places around the globe
who suffer from the earth's
ill-tempered faults.
They know.

Listen to farmers.
They court the land,
plead for favors year after year.
Some survive, dig in their plows and stay.
Others leave, rejected suitors
seeking favors in the arms
of more forgiving earth.

Ask me. My house stood firm
for fifteen years, then on some
terra unfirma whim
split and fell an inch or so,
the northeast corner
seeking its own space.

A presence filled the rift between,
then rose to walk from room to room.
She did not speak, but startled me
with her first nocturnal stroll.
She meant no harm, I guess.
I haven't seen her
since they raised the slab,
returning the house
to some sort of normal.

Linda Banks
Mesquite, Texas

Contest 43 ~ Mississippi Poetry Society Award
First Place

Time, and Again

He cannot sleep upon his hillside now.
He is among us—as in times before!
And we who toss and lie awake for long
Breathe deep, and start, to see him pass the door.
"Abraham Lincoln Walks at Midnight ~ Vachel Lindsay

He cannot sleep upon his hillside now;
Too many sounds of bloodshed weight the air
His words of declaration thought to clear.
The night reverberates with missiled fear
Familiar as the notes of life's despair.
He cannot sleep upon his hillside now,

He is among us—as in times before!
He calls to daring men who will decree
His path to be the way—staunch men of truth
who blanch before the killing of our youth.
We hear his cry, but do not look to see
He is among us—as in times before!

And we who toss and lie awake for long,
Have we forgotten? Let us sound the song
Of peace, that hope might once again supplant
The bloody battlefields, the ancient chant
From innocents in graves that cry of wrong,
And we who toss and lie awake for long.

Breathe deep, and start, to see him pass the door!
Rise up and join him, and our mothers' cries
Whose hearts, as his, must bleed in deep travail
That good and sober men who cannot fail
Too often do…he is our hope! Arise,
Breathe deep, and start, to see him pass the door.

Evelyn Corry Appelbee
Henderson, Texas

Contest 43 ~ Mississippi Poetry Society Award
Second Place

Not at Peace with Snow

The woods around it have it—it is theirs.
All animals are smothered in their lairs.
I am too absent-spirited to count;
The loneliness includes me unawares.
~ "Desert Places" by Robert Frost

The woods around it have it—it is theirs.
Fast falling snow brings on a lonely spell
As I recall the love that warmed us fast
On winter walks. Not even she could tell
a mid-March snow would be her very last.
The woods around it have it—it is theirs.

All animals are smothered in their lairs.
Oh, not like her, for they have pulse and breath.
It isn't on this earth that she has rest—
Her entombed form remains in total death.
A better poet put his lost-ness best:
"All animals are smothered in their lairs."

I am too absent-spirited to count.
My loved one's loss leaves me in misery.
At times, thank God, my mind's an empty sheet.
The present snow, though, now gives injury.
I lack the faith that she and I shall meet.
I am too absent-spirited to count.

The loneliness includes me unawares—
It hasn't the least interest in my groan;
But when snow goes away I am less caught.
"Tomorrow, know," she said "you're not alone."
At least for her it was the perfect thought.
The loneliness includes me unawares.

Cecil Tresslar
Indianapolis, Indiana

Contest 43 ~ Mississippi Poetry Society Award

Third Place

Resilience

"When I see birches bend to left and right,
Across the lines of straighter darker trees,
I like to think some boy's been swinging them.
But swinging doesn't bend them down to stay"
~ from "Birches" by Robert Frost

When I see birches bend to left and right
in stormy winds but never break in spite
of getting tossed about, I think of men
who, beaten down, still stand their ground and then
can muster grit to rally from their plight.
When I see birches bend to left and right

across the lines of straighter darker trees
devoid of spontaneity to tease
my interest, I suppose that birches must
take great delight in yielding to a gust
of wind, to bob and curtsy as they please
cross the lines of straighter darker trees.

I like to think some boy's been swinging them,
some lad who's conjured up a stratagem
for flying up and down through space without
a rocket ship. He doesn't chart his route
but rides the orbit birches offer him.
I like to think some boy's been swinging them,

but swinging doesn't bend them down to stay.
Like bouncing balls the birches ricochet
whenever weighted branches touch the ground;
like hard-pressed, plucky men they will rebound.
A boy may bow the limbs when he's at play,
but swinging doesn't bend them down to stay.

Alice King Greenwood
Odessa, Texas

Contest 44 ~ Illinois State Poetry Society Award
First Place

A Bear of a Poem

I wrote a poem about a bear.
It awakens hungry from hibernation
and sets out to feast
on whatever stumbles into its path.
Great extended metaphor
when I paralleled its hunger
and subsequent quest for food
with my own hunger to write
without censoring myself,
to write whatever scurries across my
path, to release the beast inside me.
Yet knowing my own choices,
have bound my hands with heavy chains
and electrical tape stretches tautly
sealing my lips.
I write part of what wants written
wants to call attention to itself,
but what is unwritten makes me
want to scream. It is what remains
unsaid that causes me to bite
cheeks and lips and tongue
to keep the words from being spoken
aloud in my own voice unknown.

Screw the bear. The only bear in the poem
is me and I have a hunger way beyond food.
It's a teeth-snapping-head-shaking-lip-sneering-
throat-growling-gotta-get-hold-of-something
kind of hunger.

The kind of hunger that wants to find you
alongside my path, late,
late at night, when the fog has licked
your cheeks and the tip of your nose
glistens under the moon,
your mind far away full of words
and slow sweet rhythms, your eyes

lazy at the hour, your instincts down.
I want to watch you, follow
your trail, fill myself with your scent,
swoop you from the path,
secret you into the shadows.
I want to feast on you—eat you up.
Leave your bones to whiten in the sun.
Fill my pens with your essence.
Remember you when I eat words
while wrestling a gigantic bear of a poem.

Coleen T. Ward
Melbourne, Florida

Contest 44 ~ Illinois State Poetry Society Award
Second Place

Hot Coffee to Keep You Warm

"My mother had to walk the most of the way
from the end of the Railway in 'Wyhomen'
to Salt Lake City"
~ Alma Ellis Journal—1909

In this photograph you look beyond light
spotting youngest son Alma. No hint
of his early leaving prompts you
to fold every detail of his being inside
your love. You pose, properly satisfied, husband
James at your right hand, three other sons
and three daughters in polite harmony. A fascinator
tops your head. In your lap a tussie-mussie, fancy name
for posy of tired pansies. No one appears
especially happy, or sad.

I am your great-granddaughter, amazed
by your life, not by the print, black
over white, serious intentions appropriate.

1864 is no time to travel. Civil War rips
America's seams. Conflicts in Poland, Mexico,
and Afghanistan stifle emigration. Newly wed, you leave
the Bristish Isles for God. Outside New York
flames swallow a bridge in your wake. You wade
humpbacked with luggage through ice-broken
water. Chinked cattle cars rattle you
toward Missouri. A young girl at your side
falls ill. Her empty body finishes the ride.

You know nothing of buffalo or sagebrush.
It's three months from Nebraska to Mormon
country. Your shoes wear thin. On the trail you share
bread, beans, and dried bacon with William Blake.
His father dies. William rolls him in a blanket
into a grave heavy with stones
to turn away coyotes. Near the Sweetwater,

a stream clear as God's conscience,
friend Mary Ann reaches for a cup to dip
a drink for baby Isaac. Her dress cuddles
the brake rod. She topples to the ground. Wheels
crush her head. Oxen move on. In an indifferent
grave, Mary Ann lies wrapped in the yellow
quilt she stitched in England.
Captain Hyde's wagon train scrapes
into the Great Salt Lake Valley two days before
the first winter storm. In a tent you eat beef,
potatoes, and molasses. Hot coffee keeps you warm.

No mystery why a near-smile tempers your face
in the photograph. It's a survivor's wound, not
a relic of English smugness. Like a corset about the midsection
of your joy, it keeps you safe inside yourself. Necessary
as air, it will hold you tight in twenty years
when the light of your last born disappears in ashes.

Maurine Haltiner
Salt Lake City, Utah

Contest 44 ~ Illinois State Poetry Society Award
Third Place

I Am Turning Sixty

so this time I climb the tree,
the one I usually lean against
on my walk in the gully.
It's easy, like hugging an old friend:
    that tree my sister and I used to play mermaids in,
        the bark scraping my arms,
    the branch I hunkered in, uncomfortable,
        but high enough to feel what trees feel,
the breeze coming up the valley,
stirring my leaves,
shimmering the pale undersides.
In my mind Mother calls,
Time to come in.
But, mermaid, tree, whatever I've become,
it's way too early.

Five children. Five times I lay down
and pushed each one out of my body.
I watched myself breathe,
                                        cry out.
One of them, a son, was born dead.
I saw myself carry his body
down a long,
                        long flight of stairs,
cement stairs,
to an empty cellar,
where I was meant to leave him in the dark.
You see, you have to read up and pull the string
of the one tiny light bulb when you're ready to leave.
It took me three years to turn out the light,
to shut the door.

So many doors shut now.
Explain to me why I still want to open every one.
The sun puzzling through the leaves
pricks my skin,
each pore sensitized and I am newborn.

It is the first time I've been kissed
and I've been kissed a thousand times.
If this is how one ages,
    still clinging to the wonder,
    to the child in us crouching high in tree limbs,
then, Mother, you can keep on calling.
I'm not coming in.
I'll keep straddling this branch,
                                        too old now,
to be afraid of the dark.

Elaine W. Christensen
Sandy, Utah

Contest 45 ~ Gingerbread Poets Award
First Place

The Musicians

The first, cradling her viola
draws bow over strings
in blissful submission
to the voice
the voice
that comes richly mellow

the other, extended flute in hands
breathes angels into existence
so pure, radiant and fine is the sound

together they play
in such sweet harmony
that closed eyes see
and beating hearts feel
that lightness of being
that makes

players and played
become One

Margaret Guthrie
Estes Park, Colorado

Contest 45 ~ The Gingerbread Poets Award
Second Place

High School Orchestra

(for Carl Woodford)

"Move singingly across the strings!" he said.
"Cantabile! Cantabile! With grace!"
He lifted his baton and smoothly led
us through untroubled planes of gentle space—
a walk beside a sweetly flowing stream,
its melody defining our own song,
our harmonies embellishing its theme.
Thus our conductor lured his flock along.

"Be gracious to your endings. Let them sing
softly to silence. Let them fade, still round…"
I draw my bow unhurried from the strings,
extend the arc, prolong the sense of sound,
for so he taught us—let the music run.
Echoes will linger when the song is done.

Claire Van Breemen Downes
St. Cloud, Minnesota

Contest 45 ~ The Gingerbread Poets Award
Third Place

Dylan

Troubadour,
singer-poet,
friend and comrade to the muse,
pioneered a generation,
opened the floodgate that drenched,
with fresh sound, a new era.

He touched the pulse of change,
inhaled and compressed
the thoughts of a new day,
and exhaled his musical poetry.
His words filled the void
of mediocrity.
They came, new and fresh
as sudden showers,
and pooled in prophetic oracles
that reflected the image
of neglected truth.

When thoughts scream
to be heard from deep within,
and find no conscious ear
nor willing voice
their time will come.
They will burst forth and roll
across attuned hearts
in rhymed reason
From that strange low voice—
The voice of Dylan.

Tommy Little
Pearl, Mississippi

Contest 46 ~ San Antonio Poets Association Award
First Place

How Many Can You Find?

Step out onto the Planet. Draw a circle a hundred feet round.
Inside the circle are 300 things nobody understands, and,
maybe, nobody's ever really seen.
~ Lew Welch

I draw a circle around my heart and find,
within that small circumference, 300 things
that I do not understand. I find a songbird

stuck in a screened porch and a falcon high in a poplar.
I find dozens of verbs like starlings cavorting,
flitting unruly, and taking to flight each time I speak.

I find petals in the pulse, a leafless tea made of winter days,
thousands of beads unstrung and flung and missing. I find
kissing, endless kissing, and soles that hover above the ice.

rooms with no walls, a fire with no ash, a moon
in every window, and a jarful of stars.
I am trying to say what I mean.

But the more I speak, the more the miracles slip
from these lines, and loosen themselves from these words. Damn
these awkward syllables—even the ones spun from silk turn to nooses.

Can you listen to me with your hands? Come, touch
this place at the center of the circle, feel the quickening thump,
the acrobatic blood, the wheel of fast breath, the battle of cold want.

Feel this fearlessness growing wings.

Rosemerry Wahtola Trommer
Placerville, Colorado

Contest 46 ~ San Antonio Poets Association Award
Second Place

Even Time

You may think the road is straight
Stretching ahead as if inked
With a shiny steel rule.
It is not. It curves as it goes.
The sea's horizon proves
that everything is round,
if not obviously then eventually.
Eggs and eyes, seeds and the stems
of flowers, electron's paths,
Currents of wind and sea,
Raindrops and even the snowflakes
Wheeling down the sky.
And all the stars and planets
And their moons are globes of rock
Or ice or gas and not a straight line
To be found in all creation.
Some say that even time curves
and will return someday,
like the hands of a clock.
If you can find a thing that is straight—
Wooden plank or ray of light
Or a single clear thought—
watch it for a few million years
And see if it doesn't begin to curl.

Joyce Kohler
Midway, Utah

Contest 46 ~ San Antonio Poets Association Award

Third Place

Hurricanes and Vinyl LPs

The map on the weather channel
laid a white LP on
Texas and Louisiana.
A turntable of debris
whirled the circle east.
Its edge grazed my roof,
mimed record albums
stored a hundred seasons
in the storm of my upstairs closet.

Tonight, I lean over
fresh-dusted spin and watch
a black vinyl hurricane,
its spindled eye
holding music
in relentless rotation.
The stylus lifts youth
from the grooves,
blankets me on sofa cushions,
etches the smile I used to wear.
A wall cloud of sound
surrounds,
sings childhood into the
dark center
of an ebbing storm.

Budd Powell Mahan
Dallas, Texas

Contest 47 ~ Maine Poets Society Award
First Place

Easter Lilies

Lilies float on the Adriatic,
bobbing on top,
dipping, emerging
whiter than a moment before.
They hover over the stone pebbles
that line the shore,
then wing inland toward Mostar.
Here, in the city of stone,
they gather behind windows
blinded by sandbags.
Their petals curl into seashells
to remember the waves.
Nothing is lost in the echo.
Nothing diminishes here
in the cobblestone streets,
so far from the natal sea.

Janice L. Freytag
Souderton, Pennsylvania

Contest 47 ~ Maine Poets Society Award
Second Place

Calving

The great bones of the monolith
crack seconds before
the slow release of the iceberg's face.
Its descent lifts the ocean,
sends a wall toward the frail
deck on which I stand.
Cameras click the wake's approach,
but I step back, suddenly aware
of water deadly as a bullet,
the swamping sweep coming nearer.
The ship lurches and heart leaps,
my face burning with fear.
The great hull pitches and rights,
calms as the waves pass,
and I say a silent thanks for the
captain's wisdom.
How many early travelers ventured
too close to the birthing,
watched the inescapable thunder
rise up and sweep them to the
rigid clench of death.
I retreat to my cabin,
to the engine hum that propels us
toward port.
I am suddenly anxious for dry land,
the certainty of solid earth, and
the hot sand of home.

Budd Powell Mahan
Dallas, Texas

Contest 47 ~ Maine Poets Society Award
Third Place

Sea Change

Three brothers in the stateroom next to ours
yelp, as if flying round the first curve
of the wooden roller coaster at Sylvan Beach.

You and I on our side of the wall lie still
in bed, groaning middle-age midnight moans
as the ship bounds forward over turbulence,

wondering in the dark how
a mirror-smooth sea turned fiendish,
betraying a naïveté about cruises
and our sense of measured safety.

The silver-plated trash receptacles that
at first glance we mocked as middlebrow,
we now pull—one to your side of the bed,
the other to mine—closer to our chins.

JoAnne Bauer
Hartford, Connecticut

Contest 48 ~ Miriam S. Strauss Memorial Award
First Place

Before We Can Unlearn

So far it's the physical world that we speak of:
the red Frisbee, the sweet blackberry, the small pink ball.
She points to a tree. *This,* she says. *Tree.* I say. *Well,*

lilac bush. Already the world slips from its chain of syllables.
I want to speak with her about this filtered honey light
of a late April afternoon, and I do, but she brings me

a rock and says, *This.* And I say, *Rock. Gray rock.*
And even more, I want to speak of what comes next,
of the longing that this light begets—how it rouses in me

a deep wish to lose the physical world and be current,
be wave, be invisible flourish, to be warmth that drives flowers
to bloom. I want to tell her how sometimes the body

interferes, so material, so fleshsome, so brute in its hungers.
How beyond the red Frisbee there's a pulse, a rhythm,
a tide that no words can touch, and it gathers us and connects

us to this all that is: one cosmos, one bloodstream, one river,
one art. How sometimes we get it—whatever it is—and all
that is concrete dissolves in the breath. How we're twined

to this moment, and the next, and the next. *Next,* I say,
as she brings me the small wreath of grass. *Bird,* I say,
as the small body wings past. She smiles and tries to fly—

half jump, half fall, all innocence. *Yes,* I say. *That's what*
love is like. Oh golden light, Oh luminous task of losing
whatever we think we know: Tree. Rock. Nest.

Rosemerry Wahtola Trommer
Placerville, Colorado

Contest 48 ~ Miriam S. Strauss Memorial Award
Third Place

Teaching the Tapestry

Sometimes in that last half-light
between waking and dawn dreaming—
I hear my students call to me.

They come to me softly then,
holding embroidery needles
of nighttime stars. I am ready.

Threading my five-point needle
with intricate ribbon of ebony dusk,
I sew calico to gold, then to fantasy.

Before their eyes flows a quilt
of satin squares, castles and crowns,
kingdoms that are costly. One day

I hand them the thread, the cloth,
to fashion their patchwork dreams:
Their tiny hands tangle, then sew.

They enter the castles, drop the crowns,
moving backward slowly. Alas, they never
whisper goodbye. There is no time.

Andrea L. Watson
Taos, New Mexico

Contest 48 ~ Miriam S. Strauss Memorial Award
Third Place

Ten O'Clock Scholar

No diller, no dollar,
she's late every day.
Mom works nights,
stops for a beer on the way home.
Dad leaves at the crack of crack.
So it's wait for the end of beer breakfast,
if she wants a ride.
No, she can't walk to school,
the neighbrohood's a battle zone,
gangs recognize no DMZ.
Wait for Mom.
Scholar would like a beer,
but the guy at the liquor store
won't sell her any,
says he could get in big trouble
if he got caught.
Morning TV's mostly the weather channel,
all those clouds, all that rain.
She likes the tornado reports best.
Maybe a tornado will suck her up
spit her down in Oz or Hollywood
or maybe school at 8:25 am
before the bell rings.
Wouldn't that be something,
to walk in with the rest of the kids,
without the smell of beer,
without the label, tardy.

Patricia Barnes
Grosse Ile, Michigan

Contest 49 ~ Two Maggies and a Kate Award

First Place

The Stalker: Letter #387

The telephone wires turn into black snakes
each time I call you and I like it, my God,
I am addicted to the power of turning tools into creatures
with the sound of my voice.

I want to do that to you.

I cyborg things, the computer, the answering machine,
the camcorder. The hissing sets my dogs howling
and I wrap myself around them to soothe them.
I wish they were you. I wish I could
plant cacti in little dirt mounds
on your windowsills.

They would be like bars.

I am your privilege—I create life to please you,
to astound you and still you don't answer.
The mailboxes grow humps every time I mail to you
another jar, a new quilt, shreds of paper
in different colors. I am in the desert
without you, and you ignoring me
makes me bray. Listen to my camel love,
meet me on the corner and watch me

turn you into a favor.

Mary Christine Delea
Oregon City, Oregon

Contest 49 ~ Two Maggies and a Kate Award
Second Place

Cheap Crystal

The one remaining glass
of the set we bought
on our Milwaukee honeymoon
has a tiny chip
where its thin transparent rim
bumped against some obstacle.
I keep pulling it
from the back of the shelf,
testing the sharpness
of this place on its circumference
before I sip my morning orange juice
carefully from a smoother edge.

You would have tossed it away,
used one of the dozens
of other tumblers in the cupboard.
But it is my reminder
of the fragility of love, the sting
of clear, crisp words
tossed out in everyday proximity,
butting the boundaries of our lives.
I touch the rough edge,
I know that in some unguarded moment
I will taste the saltiness of blood
on lips that no longer know your kisses.

Lucille Morgan Wilson
Des Moines, Iowa

Contest 49 ~ Two Maggies and a Kate Award

Third Place

Portrait of Disjunction

If you were to paint me, you'd only need gray,
if you ever found me a proper subject at all.
The two of us are avoiding each other again
as we paddle the canoe downstream.
This year the river is deeper, and I have decided
not to be. I am afraid of becoming a channel
of sexless water deepening year by year
until I carry so much silt nothing can live in me.
"Stop here," I want to say, "I'm going to be the troll
under this bridge." But you have instructed me
to let the goats all pass. Nothing for me but to sit
growing uglier, wishing I were one of your favored goats.
At other bridges, it would be the same old goat story.
The goats always come out on top. No troll can be
allowed to cross a bridge. This is not the way we tell it
to children—they wouldn't believe a troll with heartache.
I have never acknowledged how lonely I am, and worse,
how numbly I care, so tired of wondering all my life
why all my attempts at love seem to end in the kitchen
instead of the bedroom, why I can't even risk
touching someone's arm unless I explain myself first,
while you are able to give yourself so casually,
it sometimes seems, to anyone but me.
For today I can endure drifting, even in a canoe
so full of self-pity it seems heavy as a battleship
bumping and scraping on the rocks in the river.
I know or think I might understand a little how much
your life is as full of snags as mine is full of rocks.
Perhaps that is why though we sleep in adjacent rooms,
the door between us is unlocked but never opened.
Every sentence feels like a legal sentence
to be forever celibate. Each makes me recognize
that I would trade a whole year of conversation
for one night of entwined limbs, one invitation
to be one of the casual goats who clutter your paintings.
Better a discarded sketch than an untouched canvas.

John Calvin Rezmerski
Mankato, Minnesota

Contest 50 ~ Student Award

First Place

Eating the Sky

Gramma spent her life
Eating up the sky
She told me it tasted like
The dirt beneath her azaleas
And bittersweet chocolate
She pointed up straight
To the biggest pinprick of light
And said after years of hate
She forgave and made right
Gramma gestured once more
And said that's where she
Made new friends after
Being made to leave the old
She said troubles come
And go like days in the year
It'll be light again, no need to fear
But if the darkness is scary
Don't use your arms
To cover up your head
Use them as utensils instead
As you reach up and try
Making beauty from black
By eating the sky

Josephine Ada Just ~ 11th grade
Houston, Texas

Contest 50 ~ Student Award
Second Place

Broken

It cannot rain every day,
Even though evil sits at the threshold of his door,
There's got to be something good along the way.

So many people keep telling him it's going to be okay,
Yet still he keeps wandering through life
seaching and yearning for more.
It cannot rain every day—

This they continue to say.
He knows that they're right deep down at his core,
There's got to be something good along the way

Even though he cannot pay
his rent because he's poor,
It cannot rain every day.

Encouraged, he continues to pray
for the courage to face the future, for
There's got to be something good along the way.

Tattered, broken, and battered since he returned in May,
He knows still, that despite the war,
It cannot rain every day;
There's got to be something good along the way.

Alex Stenzel ~ 11th grade
Cumming, Iowa

Contest 50 ~ Student Award
Third Place

Firefly Hopes in a Wishing Well Jar

I have little firefly hopes.
They're hard to catch.
Sometimes, I hold them too long
And they burn me,
And sometimes someone holds them too tightly,
Crushing them into glitter on their fingertips.

Whenever one gets away,
My night is a little darker
Until someone dear brings a new one for me.

I have little firefly hopes
And I keep them in a wishing well jar.
Someday, I'll have someone
And we'll set our firefly hopes free
And make constellations to guide ourselves by.
I have little firefly hopes.

Rowan Cathleen Hinton ~ 12th Grade
McKinney, Texas

INDEX BY AUTHOR

Honorable Mentions ~ 2011

1. ***NFSPS Founders Award*** – 1HM Mary Rudbeck Stanko, Canada; 2HM Jim Barton, AR; 3HM Susan Summer, PA; 4HM Evelyn Corry Appelbee, TX; 5HM Stephanie Andrews, FL; 6HM Ginny Lowe Conners, CT; 7HM Carol Willette Bachofner, ME.

2. ***Winners' Circle Award*** – 1HM Catherine "Katey" Johnson, OK; 2HM Joyce Kohler, UT; 3HM Rosemerry Wahtola Trommer, CO; 4HM Lois Muehl, IA; 5HM Andrea L. Watson, NM; 6HM Carolyn Walker, MI. 7HM none~ all moved forward due to a disqualification.

3. ***Almeda Boulton Memorial Award*** – 1HM Catherine Moran, AR; 2HM Jay D. Schroder, OR; 3HM Melody Jane Moore, CT; 4HM John McBride, IA; 5HM Robert LeFleur, MN; 6HM Lucas Jacob, TX; 7HM Betty Prisendorf, FL.

4. ***Donald R. Stodghill Memorial Award*** – 1HM Evelyn Corry Appelbee, TX; 2HM Ron Self, GA; 3HM Jay D. Schroder, OR; 4HM T.L. Hensel, GA; 5HM Kitty Yeager, AR; 6HM Clarence P. Socwell, UT; 7HM Wilda Morris, IL.

5. ***Georgia Poetry Society Award*** – 1HM Debra Kuss, KY; 2HM Joyce Kohler, UT; 3HM Linda Banks, TX; 4HM Kitty Yeager, AR; 5HM LaVerna B. Johnson, UT; 6HM Lucille Morgan Wilson, IA; 7HM Valerie Martin Bailey, TX.

6. ***Poetry Society of Texas Award*** – 1HM Barbara Blanks, TX; 2HM Russell H. Strauss, TN; 3HM Donna Pucianna, IL; 4HM Lisa M. Salinas,

TX; 5HM Jay Chollick, NY; 6HM N. Colwell Snell, UT; 7HM Debbi Miller Gutierrez, NM. *Citations:* Genevieve Didier DeWitt, LA; Barbara J. Funke, UT; Patricia Jo Koch, OK; Larry Hand, GA; Shirley Balance Blackwell, NM; Maureen Lavender, AR.

7. ***Utah State Poetry Society Award*** – 1HM Betty Leake, OH; 2HM Susan Stevens Chambers, MN; 3HM Jim Barton, AR; 4HM Mary A. Couch, IN; 5HM B.J. Alligood, FL; 6HM Candy Lish Fowler, UT; 7HM Ron Self, GA. *Citation:* Wilda Morris, IL.

8. ***Florida State Poets Association, Inc. Award*** – 1HM Janice Freytag, PA; 2HM Claire van Breemen Downes, MN; 3HM Dian S. Barnett, GA; 4HM Larry Hand, GA; 5HM Susan Stevens Chambers, MN; 6HM Juanita B. Watts, UT; 7HM Tommy Little, MS.

9. ***Alabama State Poetry Society Award*** – 1HM Mary Willette Hughes, MN; 2HM Diane Glancy, KS; 3HM Karen Gibson, UT; 4HM Glenn Pruden, UT; 5HM Mary Cimarolli, TX; 6HM J.C. Reilly, GA; 7HM Juanita B. Watts, UT.

10. ***Connecticut Poetry Society Award*** – 1HM Ann Gasser, PA; 2HM Vera Ogden Bakker, UT; 3HM Geraldine C. Felt, UT; 4HM Joyce Kohler, UT; 5HM Lee Barry Priete, FL; 6HM David L. Byrn, AZ; 7HM Russell H. Strauss. *Citation:* Susan Stevens Chambers, MN.

11. ***Max and Beverly Keith Golightly Memorial Award*** – 1HM Rose Ann Spaith, OH; 2HM Anita M. Krotz, UT; 3HM Doann Houghton-Alico, CO; 4HM Nick Sweet, TX; 5HM Colleen T. Ward, FL; 6HM Budd Powell Mahan, TX; 7HM Margo LaGattuta, MI.

12. ***League of Minnesota Poets Award*** – 1HM Ginny Lowe Conners, CT; 2HM Janet S. Henderson, CT; 3HM Crystie Cook, UT; 4HM Maurine Haltiner, UT; 5HM Mary Rudbeck Stanko, Canada; 6HM Susan Maxwell Campbell, TX; 7HM Martha P. Morrise, UT. *Citations:* Beryle Williams, CO; Elzy Cogwell, TX; Gail Denham, OR; Meredith R. Cook, MN.

13. ***Two Ladies from Texas Award*** – 1HM Loretta D. Walker, TX; 2HM Jim Barton, AR; 3HM Vera Bakker, UT; 4HM Jerri Hardesty, AL; 5HM Janice Hornburg, TN; 6HM Lucille Morgan Wilson, IA; 7HM Marilyn Stacy, TX.

14. ***Jesse Stuart Memorial Award*** – 1HM Juanita Mays, OH; 2HM Ginny Lowe Conners, CT; 3HM Valerie Martin Bailey, TX; 4HM Susan Stevens Chambers, MN; 5HM Elaine W. Christensen, UT; 6HM Audrey Cooke, FL; 7HM Ray Feeder, NM.

15. ***Indiana State Federation of Poetry Clubs Award*** – 1HM Mary Rudbeck Stanko, Canada; 2HM Viktor Richy, IA; 3HM James F. Ahearn, MI; 4HM Betty Ann Whitney, FL; 5HM Pat Jordan, MS; 6HM LaVerna B. Johnson, UT; 7HM Beryle Williams, CO.

16. ***Arizona State Poetry Society Award*** – 1HM Ron Burt, TX; 2HM Alison Chisholm, England; 3HM Lee Pellham Cotton, VA; 4HM Dian S. Barnett, GA; 5HM John Calvin Rezmerski, MN; 6HM Pat Durmon, AR; 7HM T.L. Hansel, GA. *Citations:* Jane Couvillon Powell, TX; Sandra Lake Lassen, NC, Tom Spencer, IN, Tommy Little, MS.

17. ***William Stafford Memorial Award*** – 1HM Anita M. Krotz, UT; 2HM Ron Self, GA; 3HM Kolette Montague, UT; 4HM Viktor Tichy, IA; 5HM Jeremy M. Downes, AL; 6HM Kathryn E. Clement, AZ; 7HM Lynne Benson, UT.

18. ***Nevada Poetry Society Award*** – 1HM Jim Barton, AR; 2HM Ann Gasser, PA; 3HM Lee Pellham Cotton, VA; 4HM Alison Chisholm, England; 5HM Clarence P. Socwell, UT; 6HM Maurine Haltiner, UT; 7HM Cecil Tresslar, IN. *Citations:* Sister Rafael Tilton, MN; Maxine B. Kohanski, TX.

19. ***New York Poetry Forum Award*** – 1HM Edith L. Baker, UT; 2HM Ron Self, GA; 3HM Karla von Ammon Weeks, AZ; 4HM Susan Maxwell Campbell, TX; 5HM Pat King, IA; 6HM Michael Bourgo, IA; 7HM Janet Watson, FL.

20. ***Columbine Poets of Colorado Award*** – 1HM Vera Bakker, UT; 2HM Robert L. Lynn, GA; 3HM Glenn Pruden, UT; 4HM Jerri Hardesty, AL; 5HM Jean A. Hanfelt, CO; 6HM Robert V. Davis, UT; 7HM Tommy Little, MS.

21. ***Morton D. Prouty & Elsie S. Prouty Memorial Award*** – 1HM Judy Davies, MS; 2HM Sheila Tingley Moore, TX; 3HM Kathryn E. Clement, AZ; 4HM James F. Ahearn, MI; 5HM Jeanne Losey, IN; 6HM Barbara Blanks, TX; 7HM Linda Banks, TX.

22. ***Poets Roundtable of Arkansas Award*** – 1HM John Calvin Rezmerski, MN; 2HM Mary Willette Hughes, MN; 3HM Helen Keith Beaman, UT; 4HM James F. Ahearn, MI; 5HM Maurine Haltiner, UT; 6HM Larry Hand, GA; 7HM Evelyn Corry Appelbee, TX.

23. ***CSPS James E. MacWhinney Memorial Award*** – 1HM Janet Watson, FL; 2HM Edith L. Baker, UT; 3HM Lois Sargent, MA; 4HM Joyce Shiver, FL; 5HM Jim Barton, AR; 6HM David Hedges, OR; 7HM Glenna Glee, IN. *Citation:* Naomi Stroud Simmons, TX.

24. ***Ohio Award*** – 1HM Stephanie Andrews, FL; 2HM Sister Rafael Tilton, MN; 3HM Annie Neugebauer, TX; 4HM Trina Lee, OK; 5HM Jo Barbara Taylor, NC; 6HM Kolette Montague, UT; 7HM Janet Watson, FL. *Citations:* Joyce Kohler, UT; Maurine Haltiner, UT; N. Colwell Snell, UT; Patricia Whiting, FL; Donna Pucciani, IL.

25. ***Humorous Poetry Award*** – 1HM LaVerna B. Johnson, UT; 2HM Susan Randall, UT; 3HM Barbara Blanks, TX; 4HM Alexandra Moss Zannis, IN; 5HM Marianne McNeil Logan, TX; 6HM Lynda La Rocca, CO; 7HM Martha P. Morrise, UT. *Citations:* Darla Burris, OH; Alison Chisholm, England.

26. ***Our American Indian Heritage Award*** – 1HM John Calvin Rezmerski, MN; 2HM Anthony Fusco, CT; 3HM Joyce Kohler, UT; 4HM Susan I. Paquet, NM; 5HM Joshua Conklin, CT; 6HM Maurine Haltiner, UT; 7HM Geraldine R. Pratt, UT. *Citations:* Susan Stevens Chambers, MN; Betty Leake, OH.

27. ***Minute Award*** – 1HM Jerri Hardesty, AL; 2HM Alice King Greenwood, TX; 3HM Catherine L'Herisson, TX; 4HM Evelyn Corry Appelbee, TX; 5HM Debra Kuss, KY; 6HM J. Paul Holcomb, TX; 7HM Charmaine Pappas Donovan, MN.

28. ***Missouri State Poetry Society Award*** – 1HM JoAnne Bauer, CT; 2HM Beverly Cook, UT; 3HM Charlotte Abernathy, OR; 4HM Joanne Faries, TX; 5HM Janet S. Henderson, CT; 6HM Jerri Hardesty, AL; 7HM Vera Bakker, UT.

29. ***Louisiana State Poetry Society Award*** – 1HM Clarence P. Socwell, UT; 2HM Elaine W. Christensen, UT; 3HM Anita M. Krotz, UT; 4HM Debra Kuss, KY; 5HM Margaret Gleave, UK; 6HM Linda Banks, TX; 7HM Kitty Yeager, AR. *Citations:* Betsy Kennedy, OH; Geraldine C. Felt, UT.

30. ***Barbara Stevens Memorial Award*** – 1HM Karin Bradberry, NM; 2HM Shirley Balance Blackberry, NM; 3HM Molly Saty, AZ; 4HM Glenn Pruden, UT; 5HM Sally M. Ortiz, CO; 6HM Betty Leake, OH; 7HM Kaye Bache-Snyder, CO. *Citations:* Chandra Bales, NM; Budd Powell Mahan, TX; Hildegund Steele, NM; Gail Teachworth, FL; Faye Wise, AR; Susan Whitley Peters, KS; Betty G. Heidelberger, AR; Rebecca Bailey, ID; JoAnne Bauer, CT; Elaine W. Christensen, UT.

31. ***Dorman John Grace Memorial Award*** – 1HM Budd Powell Mahan, TX; 2HM Marillyn Johnson, UT; 3HM Grace Diane Jessen, UT; 4HM Joyce Kohler, UT; 5HM Joyce Shiver, FL; 6HM Catherine Moran, AR; 7HM Shirley Elliott Cosby, TX. *Citations:* Janet Watson, FL; Von S. Bourland, TX; Martha P. Morrise, UT; Mildred Vorpahl Baass, TX; Patricia Barnes, MI.

32. ***Poetry Society of Oklahoma Award*** – 1HM Juanita B. Watts, UT; 2HM Theda Bassett, UT; 3HM Susan T. Moss, IL; 4HM Sister Rafael Tilton, MN; 5HM Valerie Martin Bailey, TX; 6HM Joyce Shiver, FL; 7HM Claire van Breemen Downes, MN.

33. ***Save Our Earth Award*** – 1HM LaVerna B. Johnson, UT; 2HM Margaret Gleave, UK; 3HM Ann Gasser, PA; 4HM Carol Willette Bachnofer, ME; 5HM Mary A. Couch, IN; 6HM & 7HM were eliminated as they were moved up due to two disqualifications.

34. ***Ben Lomond Poets Award*** – 1HM Elaine W. Christensen, UT; 2HM Pat Jordan, MS; 3HM Coleen T. Ward, FL; 4HM Ann Gasser, PA; 5HM Mary Rudbeck Stanko, Canada; 6HM Chandra Bales, NM; 7HM Joseph Shaffer, AZ.

35. ***Massachusetts State Poetry Society Award*** – 1HM Kolette Montague,

UT; 2HM Jim Barton, AR; 3HM Jacqueline Williams, AZ; 4HM Jerri Hardesty, AL; 5HM Donna Pucciani, IL; 6HM Emma Cottrell, GA; 7HM Marie C. Tollstrup, UT.

36. ***Poetry Society of Tennessee Award*** – 1HM Barbara Blanks, TX; 2HM Rosemary Dunn Moeller, SD; 3HM Russell H. Strauss, TN; 4HM Melody Jane Moore, CT; 5HM T.L. Hensel, GA; 6HM Edith L. Baker, UT; 7HM Wilda Morris, IL. *Citations:* Marilyn Stacy, TX; Helen Keith Beaman, UT.

37. ***Poetry Society of Michigan Award*** – 1HM Grace Diane Jessen, UT; 2HM Jacqueline Williams, AZ; 3HM Hilda F. Wales, NM; 4HM Catherine L'Herisson, TX; 5HM David Hedges, OR; 6HM John Calvin Rezmerski, MN; 7HM Stephanie Andrews, FL.

38. ***Lighten Your Life Award*** – 1HM Dena R. Gorrell, OK; 2HM Marilyn Norton, AR; 3HM Jerri Hardesty, AL; 4HM Brenda Brown Finnegan, MS; 5HM Ann Gasser, PA; 6HM Marilyn Stacy, TX; 7HM Mark Hudson, IL.

39. ***Iowa Poetry Association Award*** – 1HM Ray Reeder, NM; 2HM Jane Logan, NV; 3HM Shirley Ensrud, MN; 4HM Joseph L. Whitten, AL; 5HM Mike Corum, IA; 6HM Lori Shannon, IA; 7HM Marilyn Kratz, SD.

40. ***New Jersey Poetry Society Award*** – 1HM Shirley Elliott Cosby, TX; 2HM Barbara Green Powell, TX; 3HM LaVerna B. Johnson, UT; 4HM Dena R. Gorrell, OK; 5HM James F. Ahearn, MI; 6HM Molly Saty, AZ; 7HM Mary Rudbeck Stanko, Canada.

41. ***WyoPoets Award*** – 1HM Theda Bassett, UT; 2HM Marilyn Johnson, UT; 3HM Diane Glancy, KS; 4HM Sarah Hull Gurley, TN; 5HM Richard Lake, PA; 6HM Barbara Kalm, IA; 7HM Don Shook, TX. *Citations:* Jean Calkins, NC; Shirley Balance Blackwell, NM; Larry Hand, GA; Linda Schofield, OH.

42. ***Nebraska State Poetry Society Award*** – 1HM Margo LaGattuta, MI; 2HM Melody Jame Moore, CT; 3HM Caroline Johnson, IL; 4HM Pauline Mounsey, AZ; 5HM Rosemary Dunn Moeller, SD; 6HM Grace Diane Jessen, UT; 7HM Arthur G. Elser, CO.

43. ***Mississippi Poetry Society Award*** – 1HM Ruth F. Harrison, OR; 2HM Barbara J. Funke, UT; 3HM Susan Whitley Peters, KS; 4HM Lee Pelham Cotton, VA; 5HM Barbara Blanks, TX; 6HM Russell H. Strauss, TN: 7HM J. Paul Holcomb, TX.

44. ***Illinois State Poetry Society Award*** – 1HM LaVerna B. Johnson, UT; 2HM Alice E. Gross, CT; 3HM Shirley Balance Blackwell, NM; 4HM Pat King, IA; 5HM Donna Pucciani, IL; 6HM Darleen Butler, IN; 7HM Charmaine Pappas Donovan, MN.

45. ***Gingerbread Poets Award*** – 1HM Christine Beck, CT; 2HM Elizabeth Lackmann, NM; 3HM Emery L. Campbell, GA; 4HM Beth Staas, IL; 5HM Shirley Ensrud, MN; 6HM Valerie Martin Bailey, TX; 7HM Maurine

Haltiner, UT.

46. ***San Antonio Poets Association Award*** – 1HM John Calvin Rezmerski, MN; 2HM Eleanor Berry, OR; 3HM Constance Chambers, CT; 4HM Mary Cimarolli, TX; 5HM Mary Christine Delea, OR; 6HM Constance Chambers, CT; 7HM Janet Watson, FL.

47. ***Maine Poets Society Award*** – 1HM Charlotte Abernathy, OR; 2HM Maurine Haltiner, UT; 3HM Anthony Fusco, CT; 4HM Annie Neugebauer, TX; 5HM Eleanor Berry, OR; 6HM Karen Gibson, UT; 7HM Mary Christine Delea, OR.

48. ***Miriam S. Strauss Memorial Award*** – 1HM Helen Keith Beaman, UT; 2HM Michael Bourgo, IA; 3HM Julie Nelson, UT; 4HM Janet Watson, FL; 5HM Martha P. Morrise, UT; 6HM Susan Whitley Peters, KS; 7HM Donna Pucciani, IL.

49. ***Two Maggies and a Kate Award*** – 1HM Polly Opsahl, MI; 2HM Loretta Diane. Walker, TX; 3HM Robert L. Lynn, GA; 4HM Viktor Tichy, IA; 5HM Doris Stengel, MN; 6HM Meredith R. Cook, MN; 7HM Debra Kuss, KY.

50. ***Student Award*** – 1HM Olivia Niles, TX; 2HM Nicole Hunt, TX; 3HM Nicole Clark, CA; 4HM Lila Cutter, IA; 5HM Meghana Vuyyuru, TX; 6HM BreeAnn Moerbe, TX; 7HM Antony Jenkins, TX.

"Poetry lifts the veil from the hidden beauty of the world, and makes familiar objects be as if they were not familiar."

Percy Bysshe Shelley
English Poet (1792-1822)